Polly J. Fry is a prize-winning writer living on the Isle of Wight. She writes both fiction and non-fiction (under a variety of different names). This is her third collection of stories.

ALSO BY POLLY J. FRY

Wyddershyns
Unexpected Life Stories

Mrs Khan and the WI Bucket List

Voices

Am I My Voice?
Extracted and revised from Voices

WWTB'S ECOBOOKS FOR CHILDREN

The Robin Who Lost His Song
A story book for colouring

Tintom and the Stripey Jumper

Inspirations

A further collection of short stories
and Flash Fiction

by
POLLY J. FRY

Illustrated by
BARRY ECUYER

RHR

Published by
RHR
8 Brancepeth Place, Buckhurst Hill, Essex, IG9 5JL

First published 2023

Author contact at
pollyjfrywriter@gmail.com

Cover design by Alison Finch

TO

Linda Colin
David Corkhill
&
Olive Harper

without whom I would never
have started to write.

CONTENTS

INTRODUCTION

Those of you who read Voices will know that I had no intention of writing any more fiction, so this book will come as a surprise. It came about because there were many stories still on the computer and I was asked to write even more. This volume is the result of those efforts. It really will be the last fiction – too many other projects are in motion to be able to spend the time. But, thanks to all of you who've read my work.

One of the questions writers frequently get asked is 'where do you get your ideas from?' The truthful answer is 'I haven't a clue' but it's usually possible to identify something that sparks a train of thought leading to a piece of writing. So, I figured that with this final selection of pieces, I'd introduce each one with a short explanation of how it arose. The 'inspirational sayings' separating the stories have no direct link to any of them. They're just some of the things I like to put on my fridge door to keep me on the straight and narrow.

Creative writing was a very late addition to my life, having had parallel careers as a musician and mental health professional and I regarded it as a bit of fun when I did eventually put pen to paper. I'd done a lot of academic writing but my imagination never got the chance to have its day and I wasn't expecting it to be much good when it did. However, my work was received well and it was gratifying to know that someone out there enjoyed it.

So, I hope you enjoy the stories in this volume and a small insight will be given into the writer's mind, or at least, mine. I hope your own doesn't end up boggling too much as a result.

It's a wonderful thing to be able to create your own world whenever you want to.

Woody Allen

My good friend Ros belongs to a Writers' Group. One of the exercises they were given was to write a piece based on a photograph.

In her photo box, she found a picture of her grandmother pushing her mother along in a pushchair. She was chatting amiably to a woman Ros described as 'handsome', whose clothes were very masculine. At that time, it was unusual for women to dress in this fashion and it prompted Ros to wonder who the woman was and how she was related to her grandmother.

Ros's description of this woman sparked this piece of flash fiction.

FELLOW TRAVELLERS

She couldn't be considered pretty. No, the woman sitting opposite me on the train was too striking for that. Handsome; that was the word. Her gunmetal hair was tied back in an elegant bun serving to emphasise the intelligent eyes, which could only be described as violet. Who was that film star of yesteryear with eyes they called violet? Hedy Lamar? Elizabeth Taylor? But they were both beautiful and she wasn't. Her demeanour was too severe for that, her skin too pristine and forbidding. The cut of her jacket suggested she was on her way to seal an important business deal or maybe she was a doctor en route to an important conference where she'd give a paper on the new technique she'd developed to save someone's sight. Or possibly she was off to meet her lover, a rare moment of respite from a demanding career that left her little time for fripperies.

She barely glanced at me. Why would she? My own journey was taking me to a dressing down on the poor performance of my students at GCSE. I turned to the refreshment trolley and chose a chocolate bar and cup of tea.

'Blimey, Sunshine,' she cawed, 'You run aht of bleedin' doughnuts agen? You'd fink wiv a samwidge rahnd o' me own, I'd remember to bring a packed lunch.'

A cockney myself – one of a vanishing breed - I was delighted to share the table with a fellow traveller.

I spent AGES looking for a gardener to no avail and looking out onto my garden during the first Covid lockdown, I wondered how it would be if someone just popped a head round the corner and asked if I wanted help.

I now have a terrific gardener and am just hoping he never decides to retire.

ALBERT'S GARDEN

It was such a lucky break to find Albert, or more accurately, that he found her. She'd had loads of gardeners, but they'd all left because the jobs weren't big enough, they'd got too old, they'd taken a job stacking shelves so that they wouldn't be subject to seasonal change – you know the sort of thing. The local papers yielded no leads, neither did adverts in the shops, word of mouth, posters in the supermarkets – not a hope. All the gardeners employed by friends had been with them for years and were cutting down on work, not adding to it. So, she was taken by surprise when she was outside cleaning the bird feeders and he appeared from round the corner.

'I understand you be looking for a gardener,' he said.

'Most certainly. Who told you?' she asked

'The lady down the road. I used to work 'ere afore you moved in, so I knows the soil and the climate. I see that ivy's taken off again. Bet you gets loads of little birds in that.'

They were clearly on the same wavelength. 'Oh please don't let him change his mind!' she thought. 'Well, it's only small and there's not that much to do,' she said out loud. 'I've made it as self-caring as I possibly could, but if you're interested, I'd be delighted. What do you charge?'

'Better if you pays in kind' - oh-oh - 'A cup of tea and a sandwich or piece of cake, and maybe I could bring some gardening clothes to be washed once in a while. That'd do me fine. Don't want the hassle of wages at my time of life, but if we're helping each other out, well, it's different. No-one can't argue with that now, can they?'

The fact is the garden was a bit of a mess. 'Self-caring' had turned into 'overgrown and unkempt', but boy, was Albert a grafter! Gifted, too. In no time he had the beds looking beautiful, the wild area looking like an insects' dining room, the pond cleared and restocked. He'd even created a small vegetable patch. She'd never be self-sufficient but anything growing outside the kitchen window was a bonus and it was plentiful enough for one woman living on her own.

Before she moved there, she shared an allotment with her neighbour. Until they took it over, it'd never occurred to her just how big an area that is. It was hard work and nothing like she'd imagined. Her mind's eye had pictured a couple of leisurely hours at the weekends passing the time of day with friends and chatting over tea and doughnuts. Instead of that, every evening saw her digging, weeding, watering, planting, soil-improving right until the light faded too low to be helpful. Of course, the pleasure of providing for your own table far outweighs any inconvenience caused by the sheer amount of hard labour; and allotment people are a lovely bunch. They helped each other out, shared their produce, laughed and cried together in equal measure. They were a self-contained, contented community.

Moving to her new home, as much as she loved it, was a wrench, but it had to be done as repeated ill health meant she couldn't manage the outdoor work anymore and even her own garden had proved too much for her in the end. The pocket handkerchief that came with the new cottage was easily big enough but even that became too much very quickly.

When Albert finished his stint for the day, they'd sit and have a cuppa and a bite to eat, although she always ate much more than he did. 'I guess when you get older,' she thought, 'your appetite fades. That's what people say, anyway.' They'd chat for ages and he told her so much about the locality and the people who used to live in this building.

The block where she had her home was originally one household and had been converted into three houses. Hers was the one at the end, with the sideway open to the street. Before Albert told her, she hadn't realise that the ground at the back was once part of the garden. He'd been employed to look after it all and got his board and lodging as part payment, living at the other end from her on the top floor. With the house conversion, of course, the gardens had been broken up, and since she moved in they'd built the big housing estate out at the back, but at least all the current householders each had their own garden to enjoy, however tiny.

'Gardeners are undervalued,' she decided. Listening to him and learning from his experience and knowledge, she realised just how much it takes to make things thrive. She thought she was fairly competent but it was blindingly obvious now that her knowledge of horticulture was scanty at best. In truth, her contribution to the allotment had been the leg work and didn't require much expertise.

Her little patch became a glorious sanctuary in Albert's expert hands. She considered entering Open Gardens but in the end couldn't be doing with the upheaval. 'It's a shame.' She thought. 'It deserves to be shown off and shared.'

Albert gave her a wealth of good advice on future management as his visits got fewer and fewer and she started to resign herself to the fact that it was time to start looking for someone to step into his shoes. What was interesting, though, was that Albert had guided her through the process of doing more and more for herself, and apart from the heavy digging – which should be complete for a good while – there shouldn't be any need for help. That was wonderful, not just because the search for a good gardener had proven to be less than straightforward but because, well, everyone prefers to look after themselves and gardens are very close to the heart. He'd been good for her in more ways than one.

She was in the library looking through the archive at some ancient county magazines, getting ideas for a new flowerbed, when the announcement brought her up with a jolt. There it was in black and white with a photograph of Albert looking resplendent in his Sunday best:

In loving memory of
Albert Day
1932-2006
Much-loved gardener to the Wilkes estate
1948-2004
RIP

***

She sat in the garden most days, remembering those visits and taking time simply to enjoy the life flourishing around her. The rule is, of course, that matter can never be created or destroyed, only transformed, so maybe everything in this garden was a miniscule fragment of Albert's essence and his appearance simply a manifestation of that. That's what she liked to believe, anyway.

***

'You've let this place go. Thass not good. Not at all good.'

'Albert. You're dead. I know you're dead, because I saw a memorial to you in the paper when I was in the library. You've been dead for ages.'

'Now, why's you taking on so? Ain't you 'ad no dealing with the Forerunners afore?'

'No, Albert. I haven't. And as much as I appreciated your help, I don't want it now. It's spooky.'

Albert looked hurt but honestly, what would you have done? She wasn't used to being accosted by 'Forerunners' as he called them.

'Well, I thinks you should let me help out with this 'ere mess you've let the garden get inter. 'Twas a picture afore I 'trusted it to you.'

'Go away, Albert. I've no objections to it, mess or not. It's my garden and I'm happy in it.'

Much to her surprise, Albert sat down on the bench and got out his pipe. 'Can ghosts smoke pipes?' she queried. The reply was a flash of light from a match and Albert sucking the flame to get the tobacco lit. 'Good grief. How utterly weird,' she thought.

She wasn't that keen on sitting next to a

pipe-smoking ghost, even if he was harmless and had helped her get the garden back into good order the year before. So, she got up and went into the shed.

'No good you goin' in there an' a'lockin' the door,' he said. 'I can walk through it.'

She was starting to feel persecuted. She treasured her afternoons out here, tidying, watering, sometimes even planting. It wasn't up to Albert's standard, but then he'd been a professional gardener on the big estate. Of course he was better at it than she was. He was an expert, and a strong, fit expert at that. Since she'd been ill, she had so little strength. At times she struggled to stand up.

It'd been a blow having to leave her job but a year of sick leave – she could see their point. They couldn't keep paying her forever, not when they had to get someone in to do the work in her place. It wasn't a particularly difficult job, but she'd liked it all the same. The people were friendly and for what it was it paid really well.

But the garden. Everyone, even the doctor, had told her that being out there would do her good. 'Fresh air and contact with nature.' That's what he'd said. So that's what she'd been doing and it was working. She was getting tougher every day.

She resented Albert's intrusion. It was okay when she'd needed a gardener but she was fine now. Truly she was. Her little patch of heaven was a bit untidy but nothing she couldn't handle.

**

She was pleased that for the next few days Albert made himself scarce. No more visitations, no more censure for not keeping the place as ship-shape as he considered she should. It was coming into high summer and the roses were utterly glorious, especially the pink one climbing up the side of the wall – was it Cecilia Brunner he'd called it? If she remembered, she'd cut a bunch and take them in. They'd look good on the dining room table. And the smell! Well, none of us can describe a smell, of course, but it spread through the whole house, a bit of the outside permeating the indoors, turning it all into one big soul-enhancing refuge from the realities of everyday living. On a warm evening, she could hear passers-by through the window commenting on how fresh and sweet it always smelt walking past her home.

She was still very careful not to overdo things. Another four months in hospital, with one of them in intensive care – well, it took a bit of getting over. But she was eating well again and making sure her diet was balanced. She'd stocked her freezer absolutely full (thank goodness) before she even got ill, and she knew what she was getting was nutritious and environmentally friendly because she'd made it all herself, much of it with produce from the patch outside the bedroom window; and there was so much in the cupboards – a real variety, too – so there was always something to tempt her.

***

Looking out of the kitchen window, she saw Albert there again. This was just too bad. She stormed her way out and confronted him:

'Just what do you think you're doing, here again after I told you I don't need you anymore and certainly don't want you!'

'Only trying to help, Missy,' he said.

'Missy? What century did you come here from? If it's not enough that you haunt my garden, you treat me like a five- year-old in a Victorian grand house!'

Albert again looked a bit pained. She'd been keen enough to see him before. Keen enough to have his help and his company in the old days before she'd read that notice in the newspaper; and between them, they'd done a wonderful job. The garden looked like a 'lived in showcase', blooming all year round with the vegetable patch providing tasty food she could pick and put straight in the pot any time she wanted it.

'You were happy to have me here before, Mi – Olivia,' he said.

'Yes, but that was before I knew you were a ghost!'

She flounced off, hoping he'd be gone by the time she returned. When she went back, carrying the packet of seeds she'd set aside to sprinkle this afternoon, there were two strangers in her garden. In her garden! What on earth was going on today?

'Get out of my garden! You're trespassing! First Albert, now you! Get out!'

Albert looked at her quizzically. 'Ah,' he said. 'Now I sees the problem.' He took her arm and gently led her off through the fence.

That was the last anyone ever saw of them.

There comes a point in your
life when you realize:
Who matters,
Who never did,
Who won't anymore,
And who always will.
So, don't worry about people
from your past, there's a
reason why they didn't make
it to your future.

Andrew Lindsay Gordon

The following story came to me fully formed while doing the washing up one morning. Please don't ask where it came from. I have no idea!

DAVINIA

She was so called because her parents had been unable to choose between Davina and Lavinia. 'Stupid name,' she always thought and as soon as she was able, changed it to Lavender. Bad move – it was (inevitably) shortened to Lavvy. 'I could tell everyone my name was Vinny before,' she lamented, and this contraction had, at least, given her some street cred by virtue of its association with her namesake, Vinnie Jones. 'Not much street cred to be squeezed from Lavvy.'

As she had the name, she might as well live up to it and got a job with the local council cleaning toilets. 'Honest work,' she decided, 'and someone has to do it. It might as well be me.' The contributions to her bank account, whilst not lavish, were adequate for her needs.

***

After an embarrassing collision outside the waiting room, he lifted her hand to his lips and gently kissed it. 'Pardon,' he muttered, taking her by surprise. 'Crikey,' she thought, 'surely that form of greeting hit the buffers centuries pre-Covid!'

'And your name?' he enquired.

'Lavvy,' she replied.

'Ah, La vie,' he sighed, 'and that is 'ow you remind me of, ma chère. La force vital of life itself.'

Looking out of the window from their sumptuous apartment on the edge of the Bois de Boulogne, she never regretted changing her name again.

It seems that in spite of being electively single all my life, I'm still in a position of needing to be saved by a man. Please don't ask me what from.
Now, don't misunderstand me. I greatly enjoy the company of men and am firmly heterosexual (just in case you need to know) but blokes appear to believe that without their input, my life (and possibly me also) would implode. Sometimes I wonder if I have a beacon above my head flashing
'Single woman. Come and get me'.
The inspiration for this story came from these experiences.

CHARMING?

Once upon a time, there was a Handsome Prince. He was all the things a prince should be and even owned a White Charger called Pegasus. Being a Handsome Prince mindful of his duty, he spent a lot of time in the forest looking for damsels in distress, so that he could save them. After all, it was his job and therefore important that he did it well.

One day, he was merrily going about his business trotting between the trees and humming to himself when he saw a very beautiful damsel fast asleep at the bottom of a hornbeam tree. Even though she was sleeping soundly, he could see she was exhausted and her clothes looked ragged and worn. He jumped down from the horse's back and carefully picked his way through the undergrowth to where she was lying.

'Don't worry, Damsel in Distress,' he proclaimed. 'I'm here to protect you from the dangers of the forest and to restore you to your rightful place.'

The Damsel in Distress looked up at him through bleary eyes, yawned a bit and asked: 'Who the blazes might you be?'

'I am your Handsome Prince, here to save you,' he replied, taken aback by her less than enthusiastic response.

'Oh well,' she said. 'Better get on with it then.'

He scooped her up, put her on Pegasus, made sure she was sitting securely and took her down to the High Street, where he bought her some lovely new clothes. 'Shall we put it on the account, Handsome Prince?' asked the retail assistant. 'If you would, please,' said HP. 'That's that, then,' thought the retail assistant. 'Bye bye money and bye bye clothes.' And he put the Damsel's old, ragged clothes in the bin at the back ready to take to the charity shop.

'All in a day's work,' thought the Prince, making his way back to his castle to have a decent dinner, feeling he had done his duty well that day.

***

One morning, the Prince was sitting by a small pool in the forest when a toad came along and jumped on his shoulder. The toad was croaking and tapping on his cheek. The Prince turned to look at it. 'Are you my Fairy Godmother?' he asked.

'Of course not, you stupid great pillock. Do I look like a fairy godmother? I'm a toad.' This was, as we know, the second time in a few days he'd had a response that made him feel as if things might not going as well as he thought they were.

'What are you doing here then?' he asked the toad, a bit worried about what the reply might be.

'I've come to ask you what you think you're up to. All these women you go around bothering. Don't you realise it's the twenty-first century and you could get done for assault? You might consider the possibility of controlling yourself, before you end up in court.'

The Prince was shocked to the core. Surely no-one could consider he was doing anything underhand or suspect. He was simply doing his duty to shield vulnerable damsels, that was all.

'Take a look around you,' said the toad. 'Women have careers and own houses. They bring up families, share allotments and mend cars. They can take care of their own needs. They WANT you chaps, of course they do and quite possibly more than ever they did but they don't require you to step in and take over. There's loads you could do to fill your time really usefully. The world's in a sorry state and could do with any help available. Leave the girls alone, or at least, have them as friends, not projects. And stop kidnapping them, even if you do put them back where you found them.' The toad hopped off to get on with his toady business for the day, hoping he'd made the Handsome Prince see sense. 'Fat chance,' he croaked to himself. 'Well, I've done my bit. Now it's up to him.'

The poor Prince went home that afternoon feeling rather dejected. After all, his life had been devoted to doing good work and if he couldn't do that anymore, what was the point?

Sleep that night was troubled. His usually pleasant dreams were interrupted by thoughts that he'd been a bad prince after all, in spite of having tried so hard to do the work for which he'd been trained as well as he possibly could. After a meagre breakfast of eggs, tomatoes, mushrooms, bubble and squeak, toast, coffee and a blueberry muffin, the Handsome Prince went out into the forest on his beautiful Charger again.

'Come on, Pegasus,' he said to the horse.

'Let's see if there's anything useful we can do,' although he didn't really believe they'd find anything. 'There aren't even any dragons anymore,' he told the Charger. 'And even if there were, I wouldn't be able to slay them because I'm a vegetarian now, almost a vegan.'

Having journeyed deep into the forest, he spied a group of people milling around and making notes on their clipboards. He rode up to them and gave them a friendly salute.

'Who are you?' he asked.

'We're the Forest Conservators,' replied the man, who looked very business-like and a no-nonsense sort of chap.

'What are you doing?'

'We're monitoring what's here on the forest floor, so that we can see if the flora and fauna are coping with climate change,' said the man.

'Can I help?' asked the Prince.

'Of course you can. We're always happy to welcome newcomers.' And the man gave him an identification chart and a clipboard of his own, but best of all, a high-vis jacket with FC in large, dark blue writing on the back. This made the Prince feel official and important. It wasn't that easy to tell which plants were which, but he did his best and by the time the Conservators finished their work for the day, he felt as if he'd learned something useful.

When he got home that evening, the Prince felt pleasantly tired and flopped down on his throne with a contented smile on his face. 'I've enjoyed today,' he told no-one in particular. 'I think I'll have another go tomorrow.'

***

He spent quite a lot of time with the Forest Conservators (running into weeks) getting to know them well and coming to admire the things they did. 'How do you manage to live?' he asked one afternoon, while they were drinking tea and munching Welsh cakes made early that morning by one of the group.

'We have small huts on the far side of the forest. There's a plot where we grow our food and what's left we sell so that we can buy old clothes to alter or repair for wearing round the village. We're given things we're unable to grow but there's not much of that. Our kitchen garden is very productive. We find we have all we need and often more.'

The Prince was surprised by this answer but he'd heard that there were all sorts of people in the world and these must be some of those who were very different from the ones he was used to. On the way home (where he now travelled on foot, Pegasus preferring to live with the Conservators than at the

Palace) he bumped into a woman walking towards him on her own. The Woman looked at him warily.

'Do I know you?' she asked. The Prince recognised her as the Damsel in Distress he had rescued from beneath the hornbeam tree, even though she was wearing worn out, raggedy clothes again.

'I shouldn't think so,' he said, being careful not to tell an outright lie.

'It's just that you remind me of some prat who woke me up while I was having a nap. I'd spent the whole day foraging for mushrooms to make us all a hearty soup for the evening meal. I needed a rest. When we got back from a totally futile shopping trip, someone had nicked the trug. At least I managed to recycle the clothing he gave me. I made dish cloths and aprons out of it, so it wasn't completely wasted.' The Prince hurriedly assured her that her 'saviour's' behaviour was totally unacceptable in this day and age and, indeed, utterly incomprehensible.

'Good,' she told him, nodding and smiling at him in a friendly fashion. 'What a handsome fellow he is,' she thought, 'and not a bit like the examples of Primitive Man we often get out here in the forest.'

'Would you like to come to the hut for a cuppa and some home baked bread and damson jam?' she enquired. The Prince said yes, he would, and the two struck up an easy friendship (some might say a Friendship with Benefits, only this isn't that kind of story) and they talked about all manner of things, like string theory, how to make the perfect scone, T.S. Elliot – a comprehensive range of topics that engaged them both. The Prince's horizons were broadening daily to match the new width of his smile.

He joined the Conservators and they helped him construct a hut, where he could live amongst them and spend his time watching things grow and thrive. There were teething difficulties, of course, because it wasn't the life he was used to and they could sense he was a bit out of his depth, but they all helped each other and after a bit, the Prince settled in and became a useful member of their little community. The woman taught him how to sow seeds and nurture them while they were growing, so they became strong, healthy plants. One of the men showed him how to take a piece of clothing apart and prepare the fabric so that something useful could made from it. Another showed him how to mill different seeds into flour so it could be made into bread and other nourishing food. He even learned how to play the guitar, although he didn't think he'd ever be as proficient as his teacher. The man who'd introduced him to the Conservators turned out to be quite a famous scientist and spent a lot of time away, travelling all over the place on his bicycle to give talks about the work they were doing in the forest. There were times when they disagreed, but what else can anyone expect when there are lots of different personalities together in a small space? It never led to any real disharmony. 'So unlike life at Court,' thought the Prince. 'How refreshing.'

***

Out of the blue, while he was out litter picking one day, a black bag in one hand and a grabber in the other, another prince came riding up to him.

'So this is where you've been hiding, Cousin,' said the second prince, who was nowhere near as handsome as ours. 'What the devil do you think you're doing?'

'I'm living here doing good, useful work and making a contribution,' the Handsome Prince answered.

'Not much longer, you're not. We're clearing this part of the forest so we can build fifty homes for holidaymakers to live in.'

The Handsome Prince was horrified and outraged. 'Well, you can forget that. You can convert my castle. That'll house a hundred families and I don't need it anymore. I live here now,' he said.

'Get real, Cousin. This isn't the life you were bred for.'

'I don't give a bugger,' said our prince. 'Sod off and get the paperwork ready. I don't want to see you again until you bring the stuff for me to sign so you can convert the Castle. I'll even pay for the renovations.'

The second prince headed off and didn't return for a few weeks, so long, in fact, that they'd all forgotten he'd ever been there. When he turned up again with all the bits and pieces for the Handsome Prince to sign, HP was quite happy to do whatever was required, although he read all the small print to be sure no-one was pulling a fast one. He knew that he'd found the life he wanted to make his own and never even thought of going back to the castle and in the end, it was turned into flats and houses so that a hundred families and fifty single people could live there instead of one prince; and there wasn't even any need to build on the beautiful grounds, which were left intact for the residents to enjoy. His own hut was easily big enough for himself, and they'd extended the woman's hut so that there was enough room for a nursery. The whole community took it in turns to take care of the baby and they each took their turn in overseeing the crèche while the parents worked.

In fact, the Prince, the woman and the child, as well as the Conservators and all the people in the lovely new homes on Castle Estate lived happily ever after. The Prince had never been happier.

***

Moral of the story : next time you want to save someone, ask yourself who it really is you're rescuing; but of course, if you have a different moral of your own, that's completely fine.

Life is short.
Break the Rules.
Forgive quickly,
Kiss slowly.
Love truly.
Laugh uncontrollably
And never regret
ANYTHING
That makes you smile.

Mark Twain

I've always been interested in the way the body and mind interact and work with each other. It seems self-evident; and that there should ever have been a divide never sat well.
In recent times, I've been doing extra reading, some of it in the form of published books, other bits as papers appearing in scientific literature.

It seems to me that we got it wrong for far too long and in many ways, we still are.

Note: The following is not totally up to date, but it IS a story and less than 250 words at that!

IN THE OLD FASHIONED WAY

Once upon a time, there was no separation between mind and body. Medicine men and lay folk alike knew that our minds influenced the way our bodies functioned and our bodies worked their magic on our minds. Then, from nowhere, came René Descartes. René said all sorts of clever things, like 'Conquer yourself, not the world' and 'To know what people think, observe what they do, not what they say', so when he argued that mind and body are two different entities, people sat up and listened, and for four hundred years we had Cartesian Dualism, when in spite of life getting better and easier, people got iller and iller and lots of clever people couldn't work out why health was getting worse.

Then, in the not-quite-such-a-long-time ago, a few brainy types started to think that maybe the split wasn't that straightforward after all. Scientists began looking more closely at things like neural pathways and immunology and they could see how what happens in the brain gets expressed in the body and vice versa. But, because so much was known about medical science, everyone had to specialise in their own cubic nanometre of body and couldn't see what was going on in their neighbour's cubic nanometre; and people who believed in a mind/body interface were considered slightly bonkers, although paradoxically, they were better at life than the rest of us.

Moral: it's time to let all the component bits get jiggy together again (metaphorically speaking, of course).

Shall we dance?

During my early singing lessons, when I was eighteen or nineteen, my teacher and I worked on Schumann's Frauenliebe und Leben* together. He said that even though I was too young to sing it then, it would grow with me with further layers of meaning opening up at the different stages of my life. He was right. I've never sung it in public but I'm beginning, at last, to understand what it's all about.

Sitting at my desk one afternoon, I started to wonder how different it might be if this cycle was written now, rather than in the nineteenth century.

This is the result.

*A Woman's Love and Life

SONG CYCLE

The tantalising fragrance of honeysuckle drifting across on a slow breeze coupled with the rich, comforting shades of an early summer sunset are turning the evening into a sensual feast to celebrate the season. All this is sparking memories of happy times, places and – inevitably – old friends. The sounds have changed; no longer the hustle and bustle of a busy town but the soothing buzzing of bees and the flow of the river. How strange that we adapt, no matter how extreme the changes the years throw at us.

None of this was planned but nothing ever is. We work at laying what we believe are foundations and so they are, but not for the structures we intend them to grow into. New realities overtake old dreams and life itself takes precedence. Memory is notoriously unreliable, so we're told. I remember long evenings in the setting sun at the pub on the Thames, drinking mocktails – were they called that back then? – and nibbling bar snacks we'd had brought out to our table. Then, the walk along the bank to the park, which could almost be crowded sometimes, there were so many others with the same idea.

It wasn't all like that, of course. Earning a living used to get in the way of our life together, although it could contribute very healthily to it and besides, it was an adventure, so the pang at the point of separation was always short-lived. Being away for days, sometimes weeks on end, seemed to keep the excitement alive; and the people at the airline were such fun. It was hard, though, travelling through time zones and being cooped up in that little cabin. You joined me sometimes, if I had a long stopover, as I did you, when you were touring. And obviously, there were never any angry words or irritations or differences of opinion. It seemed like we'd be young forever and we could own the world and all the happiness in it. The sun always shone and the rain served only to nourish the earth.

The changes, although clear now, happened imperceptibly, you getting more and more immersed in your work and me doing less and less flying. The house seems to have arrived from nowhere. One day I was a carefree bachelor girl, the next a homeowner with trips to furniture showrooms and kitchen outfitters taking on the significance that a new dress or a different style of hair once had. Paying bills became infinitely more pressing than an evening out. You didn't want to buy into any of that. Not with me, at least. It was someone else who caught your eye in the end and there you were, suddenly grown up with a wife and daughter and we faded from each other's lives without it even registering.

This evening reminded me of Munich and I suppose that's where all this has sprung from. I wonder if you ever went back? We always said we would but we said a lot of things in those heady days when taking pleasure in each other was our principal purpose. Is it still just the one daughter or are there more? Maybe a son or even a couple? Your life online looks stunning and star-studded, but it never tells the full story, does it.

Oh, I'll never know the answers to my questions but nothing can ever destroy the memory of that wonderful place we inhabited together, the place that's been and like the Land of Lost Content can never be again; but it's been replaced by all this: the sky, the sea, the wildlife, the friends, even the cordons of tomatoes growing in the vegetable patch. And yes, the daughter also, who you never knew you had, almost grown up now and playing the harp in her bedroom. She's never asked me about you, but when she does, as she surely must, I think I should tell her. She looks like you. Intense and smouldering but with a sweet nature for those who break through the barrier – her father's daughter, indeed. Would you recognise her if you saw her? I hope so. And I hope you'd like her and not hold it against her that her arrival here came from a chance meeting that we both regretted bitterly as soon as it was over. But not for long. That meeting was the defining moment of my life and how I love you for it. It's been tough, but there's no reason to suppose that things would have been any easier under any other circumstances; and imagine what I would have missed.

The scent of honeysuckle is still wafting through my window, anchoring me to the present while reminding me that none of us can ever totally lay the ghosts of the past. You'll never be gone. How could you be with the living proof of you under my own roof? How odd that with an ever present reminder, it should take the fragrance of a summer plant to evoke the memories of who we were. Funny thing, life.

Four years later

Oh God. My heart's beating so hard I think it's trying to escape from my chest and the foam on the coffee's losing all its bubbles, just like the first cup did thirty, thirty-five years ago? It seemed quite exotic drinking proper cappuccino in central London in those days. The café is now a Coffee Shop and quite upmarket, not like it was in the old days, when Luigi ruled the roost like a Roman emperor. Do you remember Luigi? Of course you do. You've never stopped coming here. I decided to forego the pastries but they'd have given me a distraction. I don't really like them anymore – an unexpected, but welcome, consequence of the passage of time. Who'd have thought I'd end up growing and preparing all my own food? Life was too busy for it even to cross my mind in the days of the Mile High Club and classical music. Damn! The coffee spoon's disappeared under the table. Here goes, let's try to scoop it up . . .

Who'd ever have imagined that spilling coffee over your trousers could lead where it did? I'd probably not have noticed you without that fateful spill and I expect for you, I was just another air hostess. They're called flight attendants these days, aren't they. I wonder why?

Have you ever noticed how it's tiny things that determine the course of our lives, not the big events we plan and work for but the silly little details we don't even notice until they've worked their magic. Sometimes not even then.

Along the road is the concert hall where I first heard you play. It hasn't changed that much, not from the outside, at least. A bit dingier, maybe, and more jaded but that's probably my perception rather than reality. I couldn't believe I was backstage with all those real-life musicians looking so grand in white tie and tails – (are they still known as Babe Magnets?) I felt totally out of my depth. They turned out to be completely ordinary, of course. It became so commonplace I took it all for granted. I loved being part of your world. Not just the music but the canal boats, long dinner parties, lazy afternoons just wandering along the river or round the park with no particular aim in mind. Do you remember the tree sparrows in the copse near the supermarket? It's an age since I've seen one but they were everywhere back then. And the starlings squabbling in the trees outside our bedroom window? I wonder if you're still interested in the natural world or if events have taken you away from all that. We drifted apart without even noticing it happening.

And then, from nowhere, I had a beautiful daughter, and then a daughter learning the harp, and then a daughter at Music College. Me! The mother of a musician! How I longed to share it with you, so you could be as thrilled as I was myself. None of my friends ever really got it but why would they? They have children of their own to be proud of. Do you remember how hopeless I was when you tried to teach me the flute? We can safely conclude she didn't get her musical gifts from me! She's playing at that same concert hall tonight. No surprise, then, that the memories are flooding back.

She never once asked about her father. She told me recently she hadn't wanted to appear ungrateful for having only one parent.   What a terrible burden for a child to carry. If she hadn't been studying where you teach – one day a week, she said – she might never have known who you were, but the facial resemblance is pretty striking and she sounds like you, too. When she asked me straight if she was related, I could hardly say no, could I. She said that when she asked to talk to you, it felt as though you were expecting it but you're not blind and of course, she has my surname. You must have wondered. She filled me in on the basics of your life, although I wasn't really sure I wanted to know. You have just the one child – her half-sister, of course, Sophie – and lost your wife five years after she was born. You had to pare down your career to raise your daughter. Now she's a doctor hoping to specialise in skin diseases – not a chip off the old block then -

and you're performing again at full pelt. I'm glad you've been able to get back where you belong.

She tells me she and Sophie get on really well together. Do you hate me for keeping you all apart? I genuinely believed it was the right thing and, to be fair, it still feels that there was no other option, given what I knew at the time.

In the fullness of time, we're going to have the same son-in-law, probably the same grandchildren. How life ducks and dives and takes us by surprise. Who could have thought we'd end up as distant relations, due to a chance meeting that led to one passionate night we both wished had never happened as soon as the sun started to rise? I realise now that you must have been very recently widowed, so you probably had to pay a disproportionate price for what was – for you – ultimately a trivial encounter.

So, here I am with a cold cup of coffee that hasn't been touched, waiting for you to turn up to discuss the arrangements for our daughter's wedding. Will I recognise you?

Of course I do. Time to face the music.

Eight months later

Oh NO! I've got to try to escape again! Where can I hide this time? The ladies' loo is losing its appeal.

A woman's wedding is said to be the happiest day of her life but no-one warned me what it'd be like when my own child tied the knot – talking of which, do you remember that hand-fasting ceremony we conducted in St Paul's Cathedral? Oh good grief! That tiny little scrap who came into the world from nowhere: a wife! She's totally radiant and her husband's such a lovely guy. Her husband? Is she really old enough? Oh no. I promised myself I wouldn't cry but how do I stem the flow.

We needn't have worried. It's going really well and everyone's happy. You look so proud and relaxed in your role as Father of the Bride. Seeing you here with your two gorgeous girls – oh for goodness sake. They're women, even if they do still seem like children to us. It tugs the heart strings to be sure, but it's a wedding. If they can't be tugged today, when can they be?

43

Oh dear. Here comes the Dreaded Cousin yet again. At least he's not drunk yet. Maybe that new girlfriend's a good influence. If I nip out of the way sharpish, maybe he won't notice me. I have to admit I'm spending a disproportionate length of time escaping to the little girls' room whenever I see him heading in my direction. Is that unkind? Too late to worry now. Besides, my motto has always been 'whatever it takes.' Why change the habit of a lifetime?

I went into her bedroom earlier while we were waiting for the cars. You stayed downstairs with her, trying to calm her nerves and make the time pass a little faster in what felt like an eternal chasm between being ready and everything starting to happen. The scent of honeysuckle outside the window was so strong you could taste it. Going in there on this day of all days was overwhelmingly sad, deliriously happy and full of pride all at once. Her imprint is almost tangible; all the things she left here, so that on her visits home, that's the way it would still feel. Her very first harp, the teddy she still loves to bits – I wonder why she doesn't want to take it with her? A total commitment to adulthood, perhaps. Did I really manage to raise this incredible young woman or will I wake up in the morning and discover it's all been a dream, and in reality I'm still pounding up and down that cabin serving coffee and tea and, if I'm really careless, spilling it in the lap of the 'Fluggast'. You never did claim for those trousers, did you?

Another guest with a camera, this time wanting us to pose together. 'Mother and Father of the Bride.' How grand it sounds. My smile muscles are aching. There are so many here I've never met and not all on the groom's side, by any means. I wonder why people don't just snap away without us knowing? The pictures always look better if we're not self-conscious. I hope my mascara hasn't run. We don't want the bride's mother looking like the bride of Frankenstein.

It feels so strange saying 'our daughter'. But that's who she is. And so, so much more. It'll take a long time to unravel the emotions of the day. Memories of my own young life better forgotten; the excitement of turning into an adult, the positive pregnancy test and the joy and terror that came with it; the unfathomable wonder of holding a real, living human being in my arms that had grown inside my own body; the subliminal awareness that the days of being fancy free were over for good. But more than anything, the here and now, with the indescribable pride of seeing my – our – lovely daughter starting the cycle all over again. Sorry, I have to shed a few more tears.

That meeting in Luigi's (it'll never be the Stamford Coffee House to me) we clicked again just like we did on the 747, only this time someone else was serving the coffee and it didn't end up in your lap. A lot's happened since that reunion – plenty to ponder on, maybe, when all the guests are gone and I'm sitting at home with a coffee (almost certainly cold) and a piece of wedding cake.

Now we're inextricably entwined, I wonder where the future will take us? The world's turned upside down during the time you've known today's bride, and it'll be a considerable while before it stands on its feet again. Where will we be this time next year? Will there ever even be a 'we'? Who cares? Life's much more interesting when we let it meander along without trying to force our will on it.

Oh dear, the Dreaded Cousin looming at 3 o'clock. I hope nobody's getting concerned about the state of my bladder . . .

Two years later

There's a balmy breeze out here, in spite of the season. Two thirty-four am. A mug of coffee and piece of Christmas cake on the table, both untouched. This 'untouched coffee and cake' thing is starting to feel like the backdrop to my life. Maybe that's what I should call my autobiography.

Walking along the river yesterday, the phragmites and bulrushes were towering over me, leafless ghosts of their summer selves. Surely the wind in the reeds is trying to tell us something? If only we knew how to listen. It was quite chilly but it's the end of December, when all's said and done. Maybe we'll get some rain. Everywhere looks so dry and thirsty. At least we're keeping the market garden going, however difficult it's proving to be in this unseasonal weather.

The birds think it's already spring and they're looking for lurv. Who can blame them? Let's hope they find it. It's an emotional time of year for everyone, no matter what the circumstances and in the middle of the night, everything's heightened. The house smells of pine needles and Christmas spices. And somehow, it smells warm. How lovely to be here at such a moment.

We've had some good times together over the past couple of years don't you think? A weekend in Barcelona was an inspired idea on your part. It must be thirty years since my last visit. Such a vibrant city and the colours and sounds and perfumes all so intense. Remember following the sound of a harp and turning the corner expecting to find a bandstand and instead finding a busker? We both felt totally inadequate because neither of us speaks a single word of Spanish but he could communicate with us fluently in English. We don't see busking harpists in this country, do we? Not that that surprises me.

I'm sorry your fiancé decided there was too much unfinished business between us for her to compete with, as I don't think either you or I feel like that. But it's far better to find out before the nuptials than after. It must have been hard for her. I hope she's found someone else to be happy with. Some people are just better off in a couple, aren't they, and that's the way they should be.

Do you remember the hot chocolate with rum we had in the Munich Christmas market? I think I'll try some of that this year. There's plenty of rum left in the cupboard. The cakes didn't take as much as we thought they would. Can you get drunk on fruit cake? I guess we can but try!

The house is covered from top to bottom in the accumulated decorations of a lifetime, every piece having its own unique story to share. The fairy came from that same Munich market and if she could speak, what a tale she'd have to tell. Do you suppose she'd speak in German? Probably not. They teach English in schools from kindergarten over there, don't they? I wonder if fairies have to go to school, even if they're destined to sit on the top of Christmas trees. And how do they reproduce? Like us, I suppose. I hope their wings don't get ruined.

What's the main feeling this year? It's been a tough one, with their first being stillborn and poor Adam not knowing what way to turn. He needed his wife, not his mother-in-law but she was only interested in being with her dad and we had to respect that, no matter how hard. They're okay again now and negotiating a path through the pain somehow. They've enjoyed the run up to Christmas, too. The Festive Wreaths sold in droves. The chutney was a bit of a labour of love and the mince pies – well, who would have thought that making pies could practically break your back? But it was worth it. And she had so many dates harping, there wasn't that much time for dwelling on what might have been. Their house looks lovely, understated but joyous. You said you don't bother with yours, as there's not a lot of point on your own. How strange. I love my solitary Christmas. After the hectic lead up, a day to just relax and chill, to do exactly what I want is glorious. But to be fair, needing a bit of me-time is just an excuse. I always preferred it that way.

I started writing a novel in the summer, you know. It took shape while I was walking through the fields and of course, it was destined to be a blockbuster. The first chapter was such a roaring success it was wiped off the computer and the hard copy used for shopping lists. It'd be fun to make a new New Year's resolution this year. The usual one – to create happy memories – well, that'll never be usurped, but something a bit more concrete would be good, like learning Spanish, maybe . . . Don't tell me I'm rambling. I know. I'm trying to fill the time until I can legitimately get in the shower and begin my Christmas Day.

What will the New Year bring? Best not to dwell on it. Inside it looks warm and inviting and today is a time for reflection, joy, peace and tranquillity. A chance to be thankful for all the chips making up the mosaic of life. Maybe not so much of the eating, drinking and being merry at this stage. Well, being happy, certainly, but eating and drinking? I eat well all year round, so it's not such a big deal on this one day of the year – and being content has a lot to be said for it.

Whatever you're doing at this time, take good care and be as happy as you can be.

Merry Christmas.

Five years later

What a day! So, so exciting and everyone having

such a good time. 'The Most Significant Contribution of the Year to the Local Environment'. It's a mouthful but Wow! All this, and the whole thing stems from the lovely couple next door giving me a small plot of their garden 'so that I could grow nice fresh veg for the little girl'. Without that, it would never even have got started. What's that expression about it all turning on a sixpence? Okay, it's a cliché, but clichés are clichés because they're accurate.

What with Dreaded Cousin pitching up, it's a relief we don't brew beer or cider, although Adam said he'd like to try his hand at wine. DC was sober. All day, as far as I can tell. At least, when he spoke to me, he was. We didn't find him supine in the vegetable beds, so that's a good start. Yes, I know I should be kinder and more understanding, but I'm way beyond believing I can save the world, and DC's made it abundantly clear he'd rather not be saved anyway.

All this is down to Adam's vision and willingness to take chances. He's the brains. I'm just the do-er. Mothers- and sons-in-law are traditionally antagonistic but he's such a good bloke and absolutely right for her. It was a stroke of good fortune they had the twins the second time around. Those nine months were understandably fraught and they couldn't have faced it all again. Tough work, though, looking after twins. They were as good as gold. From start to finish. It was a lovely touch having the Harp Choir playing from time to time. Like I said before, she didn't get it from me!

A chamomile tea might be in order to help restore equilibrium. After all, that's the selling point for it. Everyone else seems to take it in their stride. Or maybe it's just bluff. So, breathe. And again. That's it. Cool, calm and collected. Well, maybe not.

It was an excellent idea of yours to have a cut flower garden, with everything in it bee- or butterfly-friendly. Visitors love it. And it's an unusual twist to the 'Pick your own' theme. Adam wants to create a dedicated educational programme for children and it's up to him, now, I guess. It's their future, not mine.

It's getting chilly out here. Where's my jacket? Right. I really must bring myself down to earth. I so wish you were here. You're a good influence on me, level headed and solid.

If I ever write that autobiography, how much of it will be dedicated to sitting out here in the dead of night, watching the moon, stars and wildlife? Maybe put something on the CD player . . . Is that very old fashioned? Of course it is. No-one under thirty even knows what a CD is.

I wonder what you're up to now? On a massive high after a really good show or all in a day's work, just relaxing in a hotel room with a book and a beer? Do you remember the time w...

No. This isn't the moment for nostalgia, but to look to the future.

Come back soon.

Some years later

The sound of gulls is so evocative, don't you think? It takes you back to childhood holidays at the seaside, when all that mattered was the size of the sandcastles, the gritty sandwiches and how long it would be to the next ice cream. Later, of course, groups of us taking children to the beach, sharing anecdotes and keeping each other sane. The crying of gulls always conjures up happy memories, or maybe it's just the mind playing tricks. Do you remember when we got thrown out of that café in Sydney for feeding chips to the gulls? We never found out what sort they were. Oh dear – being thrown out of a café. Surely that's one for the scrapbook.

The fragrance of night-scented stock, honeysuckle and mignonette are all blended together and swirling round my head like an aromatic blanket, cushioning me against reality. Exhaustion is so deep, there's no hope of sleeping. Maybe I should have been a perfumier. Whoever manages to capture that particular cocktail will make the world a better place.

The birds were out in force again along the riverbank today. There was a bearded tit – did you know they call them reedlings now, for some arcane reason? – where the drove road crosses the path. I wish I knew more about wild flowers. There are only about half a dozen I'm able to identify with any degree of confidence, even after all this time. They're struggling in the heat and dry, as well. I wonder how the birds have coped with their broods? It must be tough finding food

49

and water when you can't just pop down to the shop. What a life, eh?

The service was beautiful. Joanna even played at your request. I wonder how she kept it all together? Treated it like another job, I expect. Do you remember when you played the Mozart Flute and Harp together? Of course you do. Or Flat and Sharp, as you and your friends always called it. I wonder why? It seems like a really silly in-joke. But then, most in-jokes are.

Sitting in the churchyard afterwards, the scent of honeysuckle crept right into me, and we were walking beside the Thames again, gently squabbling about nothing that mattered very much, holding hands and laughing at our own folly. And frantically scrabbling in the morning, because we'd spent far too much of the night doing what comes naturally and had to get ready at breakneck speed, you for another day's rehearsing, me for a long haul from Heathrow. We never did get back to Munich. I shan't go alone.

I'd have been happy to stay at home but Jo wanted us all there, so the church it was. She was right, of course. Seeing your wife nearly broke my heart. So dignified and contained. Poor woman. She only had you for a couple of years. And you, after all those years alone, you were only with her for a matter of months, if you take into account the time you were off touring. It was good of her to invite me. The look in her eyes when she gave me your flute won't easily be forgotten. You left everything else to her and the two girls, which is the way it should be. But the flute. That was something else and she and I both knew it.

Sophie read that beautiful piece from the Bible about there being a season for everything. Whether you believe or not, the Bible gets a lot right, don't you think? I never knew until today that you were a devout Catholic. I wonder why you never told me? Maybe because I'm such a devout heathen. Sophie's wife's a nice woman. It feels odd to our generation, doesn't it, saying 'her wife'. Not to them, though. They've grown up with it. It's a better world in many ways. But some things never change.

Getting my thoughts in order is going to take a while; and my feelings? My feelings will probably remain forever jumbled. I'm sitting out here with your flute on my lap. The coffee's stone cold – is there any other way? – and the day will soon be breaking. Those little tell-tale sounds that say the night's coming to an end; the change in the air quality and the light. Or dark. And again, the scent of honeysuckle.

Schumann's Frauenliebe und Leben popped into my mind from nowhere during the readings. A Woman's Life and Love. How would he write it now, in the twenty-first century? Has human nature really changed that much? At the end of the cycle, she sings that now he's lying hard and cold, for the first time he's given her pain. 'You are my world', she tells him. And with that, the music draws to a close. But I have your flute. And the honeysuckle. There will always be the honeysuckle.

Life's short.
Eat cake.

Cheryl Russell
One of my cherished school friends

I came across this delightful picture online when I was searching for something else completely different.

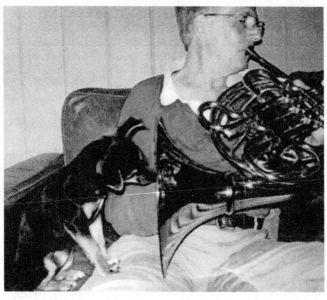

I got permission to use it through a third party, although I know nothing about them except that the horn player is called Tony and the dog, Hattie. I think all of those of us of a certain vintage will get the reference!

This is the story inspired by the picture.

THE MAN WITH THE HORN

Man and dog in perfect harmony? It looks that way, heads both turned in the same direction, the man sitting playing the horn; his dog, paws on the man's thigh, peers into its bell. His – or more accurately, Her – Master's Voice transformed into abstract sound? Or maybe simple curiosity as to where the mellow, mystical sound is coming from.

How did this picture come to be taken? A wife, maybe, catching the moment on a mobile phone or a son setting up the scene and recording it for the family archive.

'Off you get,' says the man. 'My leg's going to sleep.'

The dog turns her head and adopts a quizzical expression, not making any move at all. 'Woof?' she barks gently.

'Come on, shift. I can't feel my foot.'

The dog snuggles down, head on paws, clearly wishing the man would stop jiggling his leg. 'Woof,' she murmurs.

The man gets more insistent. 'Shift your idle bones!' he says.

The dog fixes him with an enquiring stare and what are surely raised eyebrows. 'Woof?' she asks again.

The man realises he's getting nowhere. 'Biscuity treat?' he suggests.

Propelled by energy generated by her wagging tail and channelled into her legs, the dog disappears in the direction of the treat bowl.

'Here you are, you greedy animal!' says the man affectionately, limping now on a half-dead foot. The dog, far from being offended by her master's rebuke, is delighted her plan has been successful.

A long, long time ago, I lost count of how many times I sang Messiah. Anyone familiar with the work will know The Trumpet Shall Sound.

Again, anyone who's familiar with brass instruments will be aware of how easy it is to 'split' a note and while we were doing our MMus together, my friend Matthew, a trumpeter, enlightened me that this piece is known in the business as The Trumpet Might Sound.

How this came from that I'll never know, but grow it did.

THE TRUMPET MIGHT SOUND

The editor asked: 'So, was it like you thought it would be?'

She put her coffee on the tray and considered for a moment. 'Fair question,' she replied and cast her mind back to the cosy lounge. It would have been a refuge from the snow and ice no matter what the circumstances, but on this occasion – well, this was unparalleled.

***

His hair was now completely white, his face etched with lines, but there was no stoop, and from what she could tell he was still sprightly with a firm gait and no sudden reactions to unwelcome twinges. She wondered what he saw when he looked in the mirror. Was it the still-handsome, vital eighty-year-old or the young man fixed in her own mind's eye? She'd read that we see ourselves the way we were in our late twenties and she knew that photographs taken of her recently looked nothing like the person staring back at her when she applied her make up. Was it the same for him?

They tried to decide when their paths had crossed for the first time. Of course, it was so long ago they'd never be sure. Obviously, he'd stopped playing. 'Played out,' he told her on the phone, 'and the lip's weak.' But, there was still the mischievous smile creeping round his mouth and the addition of specs couldn't dull the shine from the bright, intelligent eyes. 'What's going on behind them?' she pondered.

With a tiny twitch of the eyebrows he asked her 'Do you still fancy me then?' The smile was flirtatious but understated. 'How many hours in front of a mirror did it take to perfect that?' she asked herself, but what she said was: 'Well, you're still extremely attractive but let's be honest, neither of us is in the first flush of youth. The words 'Cadbury's Crème Egg' and 'Coconut Ice Cream' don't fill me with the same lust and longing they once did, either.' He chuckled and rested his head on his hand, fixing her with the hint of a smile, almost apologetic.

'And did you ever fancy me?' she dared to enquire.

'Of course,' he answered. 'You were a lovely woman and still are.' Her heart did something very odd inside her rib cage and she hoped she wasn't blushing. 'But I had a wife, four children and a mistress. There were other things on my mind.'

**

When she'd been given this assignment – 'Local Lads and Lassies Made Good' – it was just another job; one article to be published each month for a year was the plan. It wasn't particularly significant in her eyes. The list of interviewees had been prepared for her so she hadn't had to do any research to discover who these 'local lads and lassies' might be. Each entry was annotated with the sort of story they'd like. A bit of a doddle, really, as it always was when she didn't have to come up with ideas herself. It came as slightly more than a surprise, slightly less than a shock, when the email arrived informing her that they'd had a 'communication' from a reader asking if he was going to be included in the series. It meant thirteen months rather than twelve, 'but honestly,' her line manager told her, 'how could we have forgotten about him?' 'No idea,' she answered and in the safety of her own mind, she added 'I never have.'

Over a cup of tea, he enquired: 'Do you remember that Messiah in Paris? And the Strauss at the Prom? When I begged you to send prayers up so I wouldn't split the notes in the broken scale?' She laughed. 'Of course,' she said. 'And I remember you coming off stage and looking at me with a face like a force nine at sea as if it was my fault it hadn't been, let's say, quite as clear as you'd intended.'

'Ah,' he said, as a wave of embarrassment crossed his face. 'That wasn't because of you. That was because I noticed that Jen was in the audience.'

'But Jen was often in the audience,' she said.

'Sure, but not when my wife was sitting backstage.'

'Right. I feel slightly better for myself now, but not quite so much for Jen and Hilary. Why did you do it?'

'Why do we ever do anything?' he queried. 'Because we can? Because I fancied myself in love? Because I wanted to escape from a house-load of children?'

'Don't you care about your children?' she asked, her face involuntarily crumpling into a frown.

'Of course. I love them to distraction and always did, but they 'happened' to me, weren't my choice and I never was child-orientated. I get on much better with them now they're grown up; and I adore my grandchildren, but I find them very difficult to manage. I just haven't got that knack.' She wasn't absolutely sure there was any knack to it, but as she had no children of her own, didn't feel fit to judge. 'So why did you have them then?' she wanted to know.

'Hilary thought it her duty to provide me with an 'heir'. It didn't matter to me whether they were sons or daughters but it did to her, so she kept on trying until a boy was born. It felt like I was getting deeper and deeper into adding to world population without having any choice in the matter.' 'Really?' she thought. 'Did you never hear of condoms?' But she kept quiet, marital politics being something she'd never been party to. He continued: 'And to be honest, we were away from home so much in those days, we took our comforts wherever we could find them. That frequently meant either the pub or someone else's bedroom. When we got home, it was just a relief to be back and I went along with whatever was required of me.'

'But you never took your comforts with me,' she thought. 'Maybe I was lucky'; although she didn't really believe it, recalling his presence pulling at her like a bungee rope; how she loved bathing in his atmosphere, flirting with him over the shoulders of the others. 'I guess when we're young, we don't think of those things in quite as much depth,' she said. 'We think that life is ours for the taking and the consequences – if we acknowledge there'll be any – will be trivial. What happened to Hilary?' she asked out of the blue, seeing no obvious signs of a wife in the house.

'Breast cancer. She refused to get it treated and died eleven years ago.'

Shocked, all she could think to say was: 'And did you marry again?'

'Nope. It's like the playing really. I adored it. Lived for it, if I'm honest, but I retired because I'd blown myself out and my lip had gone. When Hilary died, I was devastated. It'd never occurred to me she'd not be the one to survive into old age or that she wouldn't get the treatment she needed in time. It shattered my life and I miss being a husband but I don't want to do it again.'

'Because you don't want to be vulnerable again? Don't want to be restricted in your movements?'

'Partly, but Hilary's spirit was broken many years before she became ill – and Jen's too. When you watch someone dying and know that your own behaviour might have been – no, that it definitely was – implicated in that person's misery. Well, let's just say I think I've done enough damage.' His smile had faded. The eyes were no longer laughing and dancing in front of her. His lips – almost famous in their own right – turned down slightly at the corners and his head, although not bowed, was dipped and she could feel his pain. 'Fremdschaeme?' she wondered, letting herself be distracted. 'Or does that only apply to empathic embarrassment? Maybe he deserves it'. But she didn't really believe it. Her memories of him were too fond to think truly badly of him and surely he'd paid for his folly.

***

63

She'd been employed to compile the programme notes for the concerts – not really suitable work for someone with a First Class degree in English, if her family were to be believed – but she'd played the violin since she was a small child, taken all the available exams and done loads of performing, even auditioning for professional orchestras and getting the odd engagement, but it led nowhere and the careers advisor at university suggested she might combine her interests by writing programme notes for an orchestra, opera house or maybe a record company. Her family wanted her to go back home, not remain in London, but the job had fallen into her lap and she quickly realised she loved it. The tiny office, the other women – and in those days, the admin staff were, indeed, all women – the hectic pace of the job, always regulated by deadlines and, of course, the tickets for the shows.

So there she was, in the bar with all the players, and being there was legitimate. She wasn't a gate crasher or groupie. She couldn't take her eyes off him from the first show she attended. He was utterly gorgeous but really, engaging romantically with the guys in the band? That wouldn't be a good idea at all. She rationalised it by reminding herself that there was something familiar about him and she wanted to place him; but she'd done a lot of concert-going over the years and naturally, she'd be bound to recognise him. So, it came as a surprise when she discovered he'd grown up in her village and even gone to the same schools. He was fifteen years older, so there'd have been no contact, but she'd have seen him around, she decided, ignoring the mismatch in their ages. In the bar between rehearsals and shows, they nattered about Knightshaven; and their histories, whilst not shared, had plenty in common. She never allowed herself to think he might be attracted to her too, although one of the other women had warned her: 'Watch him. He'll get into your knickers and drop you flat, like he has with dozens of others. Don't let him find a way in.'

And he never did but that was because he'd never tried. What would she have done if he had? She had no idea but was fairly sure she'd have been unable to resist.

***

'So,' she said, remembering why she was here. 'What's it like being retired? Do you miss it?'

'I've done everything I wanted to do, achieved everything I set out to and meeting you again like this, it's the icing on the cake. Given the size of the cake, that's an awful lot of icing,' he said. His answer caught her off guard.

'You can't mean that,' she replied, this time sure she was blushing through to her toenails.

'Sorry, I didn't mean to embarrass you. But yes, whether you believe me or not, I always felt differently about you. You weren't like anyone I'd ever met. I could never have wanted you as a momentary diversion to be forgotten as soon as the instant was over; and after all that happened with Jen, I was a lot more sensitive to the mayhem I was creating. I didn't want to leave any more debris behind me,' he said.

'What happened to her?'

'She married a banker, divorced him I-know-not-why and went to Thailand to be a Buddhist monk or monkess or whatever the women are called. What happened to her after that – well, your guess is as good as mine.' She observed that he'd left out the first part of the story, when Hilary had discovered the affair and there had been an internal scandal causing so much devastation it nearly finished his career. Not that there were any high moral tones abounding at that time, but being found out had knocked him off his perch and his playing had suffered tremendously.

'But what about you?' he wanted to know, 'what sort of life have you had since renouncing the joys of the Big City?'

'Oh nothing special. I saw my current job advertised, applied, got it and moved back.'

She said nothing of the reason she'd left it all behind her: the yearning to be near him, to feel his heart beating alongside hers. And then, of course, the uproar in the office when wife and mistress turned up at the same time and bawled each other out until the manager had stepped in and somehow escorted them both out of the building.

'Husband? Kids?' he enquired.

'No. No time. No interest. No opportunity. Surely you remember what Knightshaven was like back then?'

'Not really. I left when I was eighteen and have never been back, not even to visit. My parents gave me the house when they emigrated. I sold it and bought this with the proceeds. Nothing to go back for.'

***

Returning to life in Knightshaven had been tough. She missed the music, her colleagues, even the shopping and her tiny flat but she really couldn't go on harbouring an unrequited passion for someone who'd only abuse it anyway. The biggest problem with him, she'd decided, was that everyone liked him. In spite of his 'bad' behaviour, he was popular with men and women alike. Even his past conquests could find nothing nasty to say about him.

The job at the paper was okay. After a while, when she proved herself to be competent and in no need of supervision, they left her alone to come up with stories and let her create them in her own, inimitable style. She was never late – on the contrary, she was usually early – had an uncanny sense of what would work and produced far more than they could ever use. Sometimes, they'd print a story under another name to fill an empty space or lighten the mood. There'd be no bonus, of course, but she had enough money to sustain her needs, so she didn't care. They looked after her, though. The truth was, they were lucky to have her and knew as much. They never understood why she didn't take any of the offers from the Big Boys and didn't dare to ask, fearing that the question itself would drive her off to pastures new and far more glamourous than the Knightshaven Gazette.

But he was still there in the recesses of her brain. Occasionally, when she knew his orchestra was on, she'd listen to the radio so she could hear him play. She easily recognised his distinctive sound and if there was someone else in his place, she'd switch off, preferring not to torture herself with worries about what might have happened to him.

And now, here she was, interviewing him. Full circle? 'Full something,' she mused.

***

'Let me walk you to the station,' he said, standing up and moving to the door to collect his coat.

'No need,' she replied. 'It's only a couple of minutes away.'

'But it's icy. I'd never forgive myself if you slipped and hurt yourself.'

Arriving at the platform, he turned towards her and much to her surprise took her hand and kissed it, his touch so light she wasn't sure she could even feel it. It was like being caressed by the song of a nightingale. Holding back the tears with considerable effort, she boarded the train and having found somewhere to sit, looked back at the platform to wave goodbye but he'd already gone. 'Oh well,' she thought, 'he obviously doesn't have any lingering feelings, no matter what he intimated. That's the last I'll see of him.'

***

Her editor had been almost apologetic, almost angry in equal measure. 'We obviously can't run this piece of yours, not now. It's pure fantasy. What were you thinking?' So saying, she threw the paper – one of the big nationals – down on the desk. Gazing back at her from a picture taken, what, forty years ago? – was the trumpeter, smiling, trumpet in hand and looking exactly as she pictured him in her head. The date of his death was the sixteenth, three days before their meeting at his home in Craigmoor. The obituary was objective but glowing, with all the elements of her own article, although lacking the tiny personal details she'd felt able to include. 'I waited here for you,' he'd said when he opened the door and invited her in and as it turned out, it was the truth.

She'd been right though. She never would see him again.

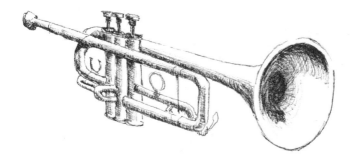

All of our reasoning ends in surrender to feeling

Blaise Pascal
Fifteenth Century Philosopher

This next is one of those pieces that popped into my mind fully formed.

THE RULES OF THE GAME

'The harp looks really sad, standing there untouched for weeks,' she said, knowing that an inanimate object can't have any feelings at all. 'Where does all this come from? This attribution of emotion to something that can't possibly feel.'

His reply was both simple and straightforward: 'It comes from where you're at in that moment,' he said and of course, he was right, but then he usually was. He asked if she'd like to go for a walk, feel the wind in her hair, get a change of scenery; but no, it was too blustery, she replied, it wouldn't be pleasant.

'Shall I get you a drink, then?' he asked.

'I don't need you to look after me,' she told him, not feeling totally committed to that statement.

He sighed. 'I don't know how to help. I'm going for a walk. Join me if you want to.'

***

She watched him through the window. 'I always thought it was men who were false and duplicitous, but it's me having the affair, not him. I never meant it to happen. It came out of the blue and all I saw was the chance for a bit of excitement to liven up the everyday grind,' she thought. 'I wish he hadn't gone out. I want to tell him how much I love him.'

***

He stood watching the waves, things churning over in his mind. Should he just tell her he knew? That it was all right. 'These things happen. We'll get through it and it might even make us stronger.'

***

She picked up the phone with caution, as she didn't usually answer if there was no identified caller.

'Hello?' she said.

'Jenna?' asked a female voice on the other end.

'Yes. And you are?', she enquired.

'My name is Roxy. I'm sleeping with Luke.'

***

'How dare he?' she raged. 'Wait till he gets back here. I'll make him pay for this.' She stamped round the room trying to calm herself so that she could treat him with the cold contempt he deserved.

In the corner, the harp suddenly looked horrified.

In the car one morning on the way to do my shopping, there was an article on the radio about the possible obsolescence of the Y chromosome, given the growing 'marginalisation' of men and the weakening of the gene itself.

As someone who loves men to bits, I don't want this to happen and CERTAINLY not in my lifetime*, but it made me wonder what might happen if it did.

*It'll take about five million years, so I should be okay.

INDIGO WITH A 'Y'

She knew she had to get away quickly. Now that men were obsolete, the Y chromosome had disappeared from the genome; but she knew that the memory bank of the Robot who delivered her son would be read and both their lives were in danger.

'Where to go?' she asked herself. 'If I'm found, it'll be the end for both of us.' Better, maybe, if she'd just offered the boy up for incineration. At least then she'd be safe herself; but when she saw him, she couldn't do it.

'What happened?' she wanted to know. 'Why did they discard half the human race?' Surely they realised there was more to men than simply providing the medium for insemination. She'd heard stories when she was still in education and there was no reason to think they were false.

She knew she'd not erred. She'd turned up, as ordered; the liquid had been flushed into her uterus and she'd waited, as instructed, until they were sure it had done its job. She'd never been involved with a real man – how could she have been? There were none to be involved with.

She thought back to her history studies and being taught about the time when there were male people as well as female. She'd found a letter tucked into the lining of one of those quaint old books, written by a woman born under the Old Order. 'Sometimes they'd hold you,' it said, 'and caress you. Instead of the syringe to instigate pregnancy, they used their own genitals,' and – according to the writer – it had been a source of great pleasure and had felt warm, loving even. But now, there was none of that. If she hadn't seen the pictures in the history books, she wouldn't even know what men had looked like.

'During the Old Order, we didn't just use men for their semen, that's a misrepresentation of the facts,' the unknown chronicler had recorded. 'We'd share our homes with them, go places with them, enjoy food together, laughter, adventures. Sometimes we'd listen to music, even make music together'. How lovely she'd made it sound. Indigo didn't even know what music was.

She often wondered where the semen came from now there were no men to provide it. Her best guess was that it was manufactured in a laboratory, but she was no scientist – she operated a computer for the Ministry of Food – so she couldn't begin to understand how it might be done. 'Not mine to know,' she decided, but now – well, it was different now she had a son of her own.

Y

In the Department for Insemination, there was much deliberation about how they should handle the situation. The man they'd taken this sample from obviously still had Y chromosomes in his emissions, in spite of all the selective irradiation; and they were clearly very strong, or else this one wouldn't have survived the post-harvest cull. What to do with him? They didn't have enough men to dispatch even one but the semen they used to grow the adult males were carefully selected and only rarely was there a mistake, like this one. They were facing a dilemma. This Indigo, rather than turn him in as the law said she should, had tried to escape with him. That had never happened before.

'It can't be allowed to happen again.' Emerald said. 'If males are born and – worse still – allowed to come to maturity outside in the Open World, the efficiency of the whole will drop. There'll be too much mingling and anything could happen. We could even end up with the Old Order again.'

This, obviously, would be disastrous – none of them doubted that. There wouldn't be the same productivity, children would be born to just anyone without regulation rather than those selected to give birth by virtue of their suitability; and probably many of them males.

'It doesn't bear thinking about,' offered Ruby. 'Men in the population again. Yuck! Why on earth didn't the Council agree to have the males removed by the Delivery Robots?'

They'd all heard the stories, not as vivid as those read by Indigo in the archives, but they knew that if there were two sexes in the population, focus was lost, not as much work was done and other countries would gain an advantage. That, most definitely, could not be allowed to happen.

Y

Indigo knew she was attracting attention. Women with babies weren't allowed on the streets, needing all their strength and nutritional intake to create sustenance for their offspring and to suckle. She couldn't hide the fact that she had a child or that her breasts were leaking. She was doing all she could to be unnoticeable but it was impossible. What had made her think she could get away with it? Everyone she passed was staring at her and surely sooner or later, someone would report her. And when would she be missed? They didn't tell you how often the Observers checked in to make sure the milk was flowing properly and that internal organs were going back to normal. If the Incubators knew the frequency of the visits, they might leave their quarters and go off to see if they could find an alternative way of life without surrendering the child they'd borne.

Under the New Order, Indigo would have two years of feeding the child from her breast and then it would be back to the Ministry of Food with the child raised on a farm – but only if it was female. Males were exceptionally rare but discarded as soon as they were identified as such.

She was pretty sure she should have started turning up to the communal feeding sessions by now. 'If another baby cries,' she'd been told, 'it stimulates your own body to produce milk.' Well, she'd never know, would she? 'But,' she thought, 'my body makes plenty, so not something I need help with.'

She knew no men's names, so was simply calling the baby 'Man'. The thought suddenly hit her that he might cry. 'I must find somewhere to hide,' she realised with more urgency than ever.

Y

The flashing light was moving slowly across the screen.

'She's there,' said Emerald, pointing at the signal. 'It won't be that difficult to pick her up. She's bound to be weak still from the birth and she didn't take much food with her, so she'll be converting all her own resources to nourish the infant.'

'All well and good,' said Sapphire, 'but what are we going to do with them?'

'Good point. She's no fool. She might even guess the truth. We have to find a solution.'

Y

Indigo was bundled into the back of a van. Much to her shock, they didn't take Man away from her but told her to put him to her breast to show them that she could provide enough to keep him alive. He drank contentedly and Indigo allowed herself to feel calm for the first time since he'd been born. 'Feeding Man is a great joy,' she told her captors.

'Do you not object to using your body to maintain the life of one of these useless males?' asked one of them.

'No, of course not'. Why lie?, she questioned in the safety of her own mind. I'm done for anyway. She turned to the Council. 'I know that this child's life is important. I love him and have no qualms about using my own body so that he may live,' she replied.

'Even though it is a male, you don't object?' asked another, unsure whether she should trust her own ears.

'No. He is my child,' said Indigo, looking at

81

Man, aware that these might be the last moments either of them would ever know.

Y

Back at the Insemination Centre, they were taken into a spotless, clinical room like the one she'd been put in when Man was manufactured. The two of them were left there for what felt like forever. She held on to her son as tightly as she could, feeling sure their short lives would soon be at an end. At least they would go together.

At length, Emerald and Ruby marched in, Emerald seating herself behind the desk, Ruby standing beside her.

'This is what's going to happen,' said Emerald. 'You will stay here for the rest of your days. You will have the freedom to roam the enclosure when not working but will never see the outside world again. It's a good place, where there are many privileges and you will be happy. Man will stay with you in your room until he is two years old and you have finished suckling him. Then he will be taken away and raised for service to the Community.'

'No!' cried Indigo. 'Please don't take him away!' But in the back of her mind she realised that if they were asking her to keep him alive, at least he wasn't going to be incinerated. If that was their plan, they'd do it immediately.

'It's best,' said Ruby. 'Once Man has been removed to be trained to fulfil a useful purpose, you will be taught a new occupation. Your life will be one of favour not enjoyed by many.'

Indigo couldn't quite believe what was happening. Why was she being allowed to continue,

82

and more to the point, why were they allowing Man to live?

She loved him with her whole being for as long as he was with her and in spite of her breaking heart, when the time came she gave him up without question. She knew that he had life ahead of him and that was more than she could ever have hoped for. She was going to train now for new work. What would it be?

Y

Harvesting the semen wasn't as bad a job as she thought it would be. Indeed, when she was working at the Ministry of Food no-one had ever thanked her and the men – who she'd never known were still around – all told her how much they enjoyed what she was doing and how grateful they felt to her for doing her job so skilfully.

She remembered the stories she'd read about how – under the Old Order – men used their own organs (not the syringe) for insemination and it gave them all, men and women alike, great pleasure and satisfaction. Gazing at D7, one of the men she'd been allocated to, she pondered the ramifications of trying his organ on herself, just to see what it was like. Surely once couldn't do any harm. After all, they'd been taught that it was good to be curious, to ask questions and try new things. And she'd never heard it was forbidden. Indeed, how could it be? There were no men to experiment with.

She released his genitals from the cage required to encase them between sessions – after all, they couldn't risk him wasting any semen between her appointments – got him ready in the way she'd been taught and positioned herself above him. 'Here goes,' she said to herself and started her research.

Y

'There are only fourteen of us left', he told her, 'and we have to supply the entire population of women.'

'But your number – D7; and one of the others on my list is P15. Surely that means there are at least – well, the alphabet's twenty-six letters long and there should be at least six other Ds and fourteen other Ps.'

'I'm afraid not. When the productive life of one of us is finished, we're just replaced – if a replacement is available – and the labelling system is continued from where it left off. So when I'm done with, my successor will be D8.'

'Why can't you just have names, like we do?' she wanted to know.

'It depersonalises us. Makes it less likely the Harvesters will want to strike up a friendship.'

Indigo thought for a moment and then asked: 'So where do the males come from?'

He looked at her sympathetically. 'You have a son, haven't you?' He enquired.

'Yes. I had to surrender him when he was two years old,' she replied.

'Did you surrender him or was he confiscated?' he asked her, then without waiting for her answer, 'No matter. I know what happened. When he's old enough, he'll become one of us, another Donor. You might even be required to harvest his semen yourself.'

'Old enough? You mean when he's an adult?'

'Depends on how you see adulthood. It'll be when he reaches puberty.'

'But he might only be twelve or thirteen, maybe even younger!' Indigo was beginning to wish she hadn't started this line of enquiry.

'It's not a bad life,' he said. 'We have plenty of privileges and let's be honest, at least we're alive. The women all believe that their sons have been incinerated.'

'And they're not?' Indigo wasn't sure whether to be shocked or ecstatic. She thought back over her own history and the conversations she'd had with the other Harvesters and it was only then she realised that every one of them had given birth to a son herself. Had they been like her and run away or had they been specially chosen to bear the precious male child to be a Donor for the future? She'd never know.

'Of course not. There are too few of us to be able to discard any. They discovered they couldn't manufacture semen – too many abnormalities – and cloning leads to an even greater reduction in the gene pool as well as too many replicas that can't be efficiently utilised. Sadly – for them but not for us – they need us, although we all outlive our usefulness.'

'What happens then?' she asked, not at all sure that she really wanted to know.

'No idea. When they think we've supplied all we can, we disappear. No-one knows where to or how.'

'So D1 – D6. They're not still in the Compound?' she asked him.

'Who knows? They're certainly not still part of our little community.' Then quite abruptly: 'Look, you've been here twenty minutes already. You'd better get on with the job they require of you or they'll put restrictions on you.'

Indigo did what she had to do, placed the small phial in the chute and bade him farewell.

Turning back to him when she reached the door, she asked 'How is it that they didn't pick up I was carrying a boy during the pregnancy?'

'They did.' He replied. 'They need boys. What they bank on is women giving up their sons for incineration without question. Some of you won't. Not willingly, anyway. That's why you're here.'

'Same time tomorrow,' she said. He smiled and told her he'd look forward to it.

Y

The Robot on the desk told her she was going to start Inseminator training. Her work, it told her, had fallen 'below standard'. She was escorted to the Reproduction Block by one of the other Robots that always stood silent and motionless in the foyer. 'Now I know why they're there,' she thought.

She didn't want to be an Inseminator. She liked chatting to the Donors and in particular, had enjoyed her experiments with D7. 'The chronicler was right,' she'd informed him. 'It gives great pleasure to us both,' and he'd seemed pleased to know she enjoyed the investigations as much as he did. Still, she knew there was no point in arguing.

Being an Inseminator was dull. She wasn't

allowed to talk to the women beyond telling them how to lie and what to do and when, wasn't allowed to answer any of their questions or tell them what the electrodes and leads were for; wasn't even taught how to read the monitors she attached to their bellies and genitalia. She did what she was trained for and then when the bell rang, left the cubicle and went on to the next one. Sometimes, she'd see twenty women in a single shift. It was tedious work.

Back in the refectory, she tried to discover who'd taken over the Donors previously allocated to her and in particular, who was now harvesting D7. No-one knew anything, or at least, if they did they weren't willing to talk.

The Council were watching her carefully. They'd never had anyone before so openly curious and they could see how it might become problematic.

'She could end up wanting more than she's permitted. She's not one of us, after all,' said Jade. 'We can't allow her to overstep her role. There could be loss of order, with others demanding the same benefits.'

Emerald, always more moderate than the rest of them, didn't agree. 'The others have had similar experiences but they've never struck up friendships with the Donors, never questioned, never wanted to know anything at all except what they were supposed to do and how to make the most of the leisure facilities. We don't want her to cause trouble, so I think we should find her something where she can put that brain of hers to good use, stop her formulating questions and trying to find answers that might cause unrest.'

'You're suggesting we elevate her to the level of Academic. Why should we? She was just a computer operator at the Ministry of Food before she carried the male,' said Sapphire.

'Well, why shouldn't we give her the chance? She'll be less trouble with others of her kind, women who also seek solutions to problems. They'll be able to engage her more fully than the others of her current class can.' Emerald hoped she'd be able to convince the rest of the Council. She had a soft spot for this Indigo, who broke rules and somehow managed to get away with it.

'I think Emerald might have a point. We run a happy community and it'd only take one trouble maker to spoil everything we've achieved. Find her a task where her mental energy can be channelled into something for the good of the City, rather than endangering its structure.' Pearl wasn't usually so yielding but it was clear that if Indigo was going to be diverted from the dangerous path she was currently treading, they'd have to do something fairly drastic.

The meeting of the Council was brought to a sudden halt by the wailing of the sirens and the flashing light above their heads. 'What now?' Emerald asked herself. With the first tremor, it felt to her as if the New Order had already started to fail.

Y

'Man!' she exclaimed. In the chaos, Indigo knew it would be difficult to recognise anyone but surely, that nose and the lips – they were the mirror image of her own. Not that she'd looked at a mirror for years. For some reason she couldn't quite work out, she'd stopped caring about how she looked once they relocated her to the Insemination Block all those years ago. She'd done as she was told and let the other women service her and, in her turn, had done the same for them – it was good for them, they were told, it kept them healthy – but it didn't compare with her experiments with D7. Where was he now? Had he survived the earthquake? Or was he long dead, found guilty of not producing enough sperm, or the ones they had from him being substandard, even maybe containing 'Y's. She'd never know.

Man was shocked and tried to draw his hand away from hers, but she held it too tightly in her own. What did she feel? She wasn't sure she felt anything at all but this, she knew, was the boy she'd been forced to relinquish. Would he recognise her? Of course not, he was two years old when they were last together – fifteen, sixteen years ago? – and his focus then had been her breast.

'We can't mix,' he told her. 'We'll both be incinerated.'

'Look around you,' replied Indigo. 'The

entire city is decimated. We have to help each other, male or female. The survival of every one of us depends on it.' He hesitated but the wisdom in her words was clear, so the two of them searched through the rubble, helping those they could and comforting those they couldn't. Lying among the dust and debris were bodyparts and corpses alike. Things did not look good.

Y

The Council had fled to the bunker as soon as it was clear that the signals were not a drill but an alert to the entire City that they were in danger.

The strike came out of the blue, in spite of all their careful scrutiny and vigilance.

'First, we must find out how many others came through it alive and find ways to offer them shelter and food,' said Emerald.

'What about the buildings, the equipment, the Robots? Surely we need to see what's left of our physical infrastructure.' Jade was glaring at Emerald, trying to subdue her enthusiasm for putting people before property.

'Of course. We're all going to need some sort of housing, a base to work from; but that can wait. We first have to give our Subjects the means with which to stay alive.' The other members of the Council were staring at Emerald. Her conviction that the priority had to be making the population safe was not shared by all.

'We need to be sure that when this is all over, our way of life is intact. We can't let something like this destroy our society,' said Jade.

'I agree,' said Sapphire. 'We have to be certain we save those who support the ideology.'

'What we need to be sure of above all is that enough people are saved to keep our community alive, to build a new future. Ideologies can come later,' replied Emerald, clearly exasperated in the face of what she saw as ridiculous and futile opposition. It was Ruby who came to her defence. 'Emerald's absolutely right,' she said. 'Our people are what matters. We have to find a way forward that saves as many as possible. Our task here, surely, is to create a rescue package.' Of all the catastrophes they'd planned for, an earthquake on this scale hadn't even been considered.

'When the buildings were destroyed, it made the mixing of men and women possible. If they get used to that, they'll form bonds. We won't be able to restore the social order,' said Amber. 'Social order is everything.'

'How do we have a social order if we have no community to put it into practice? Without people, we have nothing. Everything else can wait.' Ruby, too, was now visibly irritated. 'Besides, there are only nine men left, sixteen if you include the ones not yet ready to become Donors, hardly enough to form bonds with each of the thousands of females. How much damage can possibly be done?' She felt that most of the Council were missing the point.
It was going to be a long and frustrating meeting.

Y

The Male was sitting on a boulder, watching them approach. In the turmoil and darkness, Indigo hadn't noticed anyone but as she got close, he spoke to her. 'You found him then, the son you carried for me.'

Shocked beyond measure, she recognised her interrogator. He looked older, of course he did, with greying hair, more body fat and less muscle tone; but the eyes, compassionate and knowing, they were definitely his, and the gentle mouth with the slightest hint of a smile – no-one could mistake them. Glancing between D7 and Man, there was no doubt that she was looking at the person who had contributed the other half of her son.

'But why would they have allocated me to you, if you were the donor for my son?' she queried, not able to take it all in.

'Why would they care? They never expected this to happen.' He looked at her with what she guessed must be affection.

What would the future hold now?

Every second is a new beginning and the possibilities are endless

Julie Hayles
(a good friend who's helped me out on many an occasion)

This arrived fully formed when I was cleaning my teeth one morning.

The conscious brain can only boggle at what goes on in the Fry subconscious.

THE HISTORY OF ICE CREAM

Flo could not understand why she had been given this topic. She thought it was a great idea that every third month, half a dozen of the members were required to speak for five minutes each on subjects allocated to them by the Committee. It meant they all got experience in Public Speaking and could learn from each other, boosting confidence and cementing bonds.

'I don't mind taking my turn,' she thought, 'but really, I don't even LIKE ice cream that much. Where on earth do I do the research?'

***

She arrived at the hall and waited to be introduced. Once on the platform, she picked up the tub provided for her. 'This is an ice cream,' she said, removing the lid and digging into it with the spoon provided.

She polished it off in a few seconds flat and displayed the empty carton to the audience. 'Now it's history,' she declared and before anyone could come up with some Smart Alec question, she scuttled off to the place in the back row she'd recently vacated.

Madam Chair – otherwise known as Miranda – mounted the podium visibly flustered. 'Yes, well, yes, thank you so much, yes, very interesting, well done. So, now, now we have er, yes, we have Sandra with a talk entitled '101 Uses for a Brown Paper Bag.'

'Ah, thought Flo, 'that's more like it.' And she settled back into her seat, preparing to be entertained.

99

In Janie's kitchen, there is a big picture window overlooking scrubland and copse. She often sits there imagining what might have been out there before the wildlife took over. Could this be one possibility?

SOPHIE'S CHOICE

David and Sophie enjoyed sitting here by the window, sharing a leisurely breakfast and then later in the day an equally leisurely dinner. Saturdays and Sundays were always slightly different, because the time was theirs, not paid for by respective employers. The outside space was beautiful, if a little small for their aspirations, but the estate agent had told them that from time to time bits of land at the back came up for sale and they could expand. It hadn't happened yet, though, and it was nearly six years now. Still, they weren't planning to go anywhere, so they could wait.

This particular Saturday morning began like any other – a lazy start to the day, a search in the fridge to decide what they should eat, followed by sitting down to the first meal of the weekend in their dressing gowns.

David soon realised that Sophie was seeing it again. 'It's not real, you know,' he told her. 'What's the point?' he asked himself. 'We've had this discussion many times and she just ignores me.'

'I can't believe you can't see it,' she answered. 'It's wonderful. Uplifting and welcoming.'

He got up, took his dishes to the sink and left her to it.

***

The ballroom was massive, brightly lit and cheerful. There must have been fifty couples all dancing round the floor and she wished she'd paid more attention to her lessons. She might know what the dance was and even, possibly, be able to place the era.

She wasn't much of a historian, more of a scientist, although these days her life seemed to be taken up with chasing other people to get their reports in on time. She'd been doing this for years and wasn't challenged anymore. 'Maybe he's right. Maybe it's because I'm bored. I'm seeing things that aren't there.' It was a dangerous line of thought, as one of the guys at work had been showing a lot of interest in her recently and it was throwing light on cracks in the marriage. Her next thought was that she must get the washing up done and dress. But she was transfixed. The garden and surrounds didn't seem big enough to accommodate such a grand dance hall but there it was, as clear as the kitchen accoutrements and vegetable patch outside the garden door.

'I'm a bit worried about Sophie,' said David. 'I know she's your daughter and whatever I say, you'll be on her side, and that's exactly as it should be. But, she keeps seeing things and I'm convinced she's having an affair.' There was no love lost between David and his mother-in-law. They tolerated each other but that was the best they could do. To Anna's way of thinking, Sophie should be a mother, not a dull academic, and David should have put his foot down, not given in to her silly whims about wanting to justify all the years of study and the post-Doc placements she'd had since finishing her formal education. 'It's her choice, Anna. The days when women were their husbands' chattels and had to do their bidding are over,' David told her on many an occasion.

'And you don't want children?' asked Anna.

'I don't want them with a woman unwilling to go down the path of motherhood, no, and Sophie was always ambivalent, even when we were students.'

Anna simply pursed her lips and made her way to the kettle. David sighed. 'Can we really solve everything with a cup of tea?' he pondered. 'If only,' came the response from the inner voice inside his brain.

Sophie, for her part, was unaware of all the concern. She was happy enough, whilst aware that life hadn't turned out quite as she'd seen it in her mind's eye, 'But then,' she thought, 'whose does?'

On the train on the way to work on Monday, she thought about the ballroom with its cheery music and laughing dancers. She imagined herself swirling around the room with Jack, the physics technician in the lab on the other side of the corridor and came back to earth with a bump. 'Shouldn't that be with David?' She got out her magazine and did her very best to concentrate on the articles relating to skin softness and more bouncy hair.

The journey to work seemed to take forever and it was with very mixed feelings that she greeted Jack, the first person she saw on entering the building.

***

'She's staying later and later at work,' David told his sister, Jenny. 'She says the buck stops with her and she needs to be sure everything's up to date.'

'She needs a rest. Take her on holiday, somewhere exotic, somewhere you can start again. Pretend it's the honeymoon you didn't get the chance to take when you got married. You can afford it now.'

David agreed to give it some thought.

***

'It was a disaster,' he reported. 'She was away with the fairies most of the time, had no interest in the sights, no interest in the culture, no interest in the food, no interest in anything, especially not me.' Jenny had come over after work to see how things were panning out. 'You have to talk to her,' she advised. 'Find out how she feels about things, whether she's happy at work, at home. All that sort of stuff.'

'She'll probably tell me she wants to go off with this bloke, Jack,' he replied. 'I don't want to hear that.'

'Better you hear it now, when you're both young enough to start again than in ten years when it could well be too late.'

'But I don't want to start again. I want to sort things out and make a go of this. All marriages have sticky patches. This one's no different. Quite frankly, when she's at home here, the only time she seems happy is when she's daydreaming about that ballroom. Sometimes I'm frightened she's hallucinating, other times it simply feels like a projection of how she wants her life to look. I'm scared.' Jenny looked at her brother with a facial expression he could read only too well.

'Then you have to talk. You can't brush it under the carpet like it's a bit of annoying dirt. Tell her what you're worried about and explain what it is you want.' She said.

'But say she says she wants a divorce and it's all over.'

'Then you'll have your answer and you'll know exactly where you stand. Now, can I have that glass of wine you promised me?'

In the event, there was no chance to talk, as Sophie never returned home. He phoned the lab repeatedly but they hadn't seen her since she'd decided she wanted time off to rethink her future. Anna had no idea where she'd gone and made it perfectly clear she blamed David for her daughter's disappearance. 'I don't know why she married you in the first place. You were never in her league.'

Was there any point in informing the police? Probably not. She was an adult and had told work that she was going to be absent for a while, so this was surely planned. David started to believe she'd gone off with this Jack to inject some spice into her life, fervently hoping that the grass wouldn't seem quite so green once she was lying next to him as he snored and had to pick his dirty socks up off the bedroom floor.

Sitting at the breakfast table that morning, he looked out wistfully at the garden, remembering all their mornings together. Out of the mist arose a ballroom, massive, brightly lit and cheerful, and in it all the happy dancers, swirling around the floor without a care in the world; and in their midst was Sophie. She turned towards the window, smiled warmly and beckoned him in.

An eye for an eye will make the whole world blind.

Usually attributed to
Mahatma Ghandi

Outside the window of a flat in Cardiff where I was staying, there appeared one morning a pair of men's pants. On my return, there was another on the grass outside the supermarket. A few days later, the friend I'd been away with sent me a photograph of yet another close to where she lives.

How did they get there?

THE CURIOUS CASE...
...of the spontaneously generating grundies

Lyra was mystified. What was going on? This was the third pair of discarded men's underpants she'd walked past in the last two hours. Was there something she didn't know about? Was she just out of touch, although surely that couldn't be the case. She taught 16-18 year olds in a further education college. Undoubtedly she'd have heard. 'At least they're not Y-fronts,' she thought. 'They remind me of my dad.'

In the staff room, she gently enquired if anyone had noticed anything relating to the Great Outdoors and men's underwear. 'Is it that long, Lyra?' asked Ruth, an undercurrent of unpleasantness in her tone. 'Hallucinating?' She said, with a smirk.

'I noticed a pair about a week ago on the green,' replied James, coming to Lyra's rescue. If she was talking about this strange phenomenon, then he should too, as it bothered him. 'I can't see how a bloke can lose his undercrackers without noticing.

On the ship, Zalika was looking pleased with herself. 'These human males are certainly more interesting without the layer of skin they have round their generative organs. I think in future, we'll jettison it when we check the men in.'

***

109

It came as something of a surprise when a pair of yellow underpants with the slogan 'Restricted Entry' printed on the front landed right in front of Ruth as she was opening her front door. 'Right. Waste not, want not,' she decided and picked them up to hand over to her brother.

I'm very fortunate in that I've never had to negotiate marital politics, for which I will be eternally grateful. I guess the process is easier for some than for others.

CHESS

You know that expression about playing chess with a pigeon? The one that says it's like arguing with an idiot - no matter how good you are, the bird will shit on the board and strut around like it won anyway? That's how Mia thought of Ross. He wasn't an idiot, far from it, but his thoughts always followed a perfectly straight trajectory with no side steps to left or right even being thinkable. Although you could see the logic in his arguments, they didn't allow for human nature, which is often less than logical in its expression; and no matter how bizarre his solutions seemed to the outside world, as far as he was concerned, they brooked no challenge.

For example, that time they decided to go to Dufton Park. He was right, of course. Taking two buses would get them there in a straight line and that clearly was the shortest route; but taking one bus meant that they didn't have to change and the journey would be prettier. It was cheaper, too, because their passes didn't cover the little single decker that was run by a privately owned company. And that other occasion, when he'd said they'd be better off going to see Ava and Leo at home in the evening, because that's when they'd both be in, meaning it'd be one meeting instead of two. He was right in that respect, no doubt about it. It definitely would save time and petrol and make for less organisation, but the entire world knew they barely spoke to each other anymore and the atmosphere would be impossible. So better, surely, to arrange to see them separately on neutral ground, so they could talk things over properly. But no. 'You know I'm right,' he said, his face wearing that fixed expression that told the world he'd won the argument fair and square.

She'd found it quite an attractive trait in the beginning. It was good to be around someone who knew his own mind, rather than having to deliberate all the time (like she did herself) resulting in indigestion from the trauma of trying to find the right answer. But the current dilemma, well, that was different.

Watching the various water birds scrabble around for food on the lake, she tried to decide what the most logical solution would be. Without doubt, that would be his approach and if she could find ways of fleshing it out, so that the empathic solution could be incorporated into the most direct one, well, that'd make perfect sense and they'd both be happy.

Or would they? She often wondered if Ross was genuinely happy or if he looked at the circumstances of his life – lovely home, good job, nice wife (or so she hoped) - and decided that the correct response was 'happiness', so that was his interpretation of the facts and he proceeded on the basis of 'The facts tell me I should be happy, so I am'.

She threw some more bird pellets into the lake for the ducks to squabble over. There was something to be said for taking the simplest, least convoluted route. 'I mean, just look at these birdies,' she thought. 'They don't deliberate over whether it's best to search around on the banks finding their own titbits or eat the food provided, so they don't have to push the others out of the way and risk injury and all sorts. They just see the stuff we throw for them and go for it. They're thriving, that's for sure.'

But, she couldn't stay there all day. There were places to go, people to see. She preferred working part-time, even though she thought she'd hate it. He'd been right in that instance. 'What's the point of you putting all those hours in when you've got so many interests you want to pursue?' he wanted to know. 'You've always said you want more time, so that you can devote more energy to leisure. We'll manage. There are always ways we can spend less. Fewer holidays for a start. Better to be content all year round than have to force it all into a few weeks of the year, which might turn out to be a disaster anyway.' So she'd asked to cut her hours by a half and whilst it was clear that they were doing her a massive favour ('It costs more to employ two people part-time than one full-timer, Mrs Jackson') after a period of negotiation, they'd agreed and it was working well all round. Two employees might be more expensive, but they came up with more than twice the ideas and always worked far more than their contracted time, so the company gained; and both of them were fresh and invigorated when they came back to work after their days off. Why had it taken so long to come round to the idea?

She hadn't done as much with her hobbies as she thought she might – the painting of the lake was still unfinished after all this time; and the coat she was making, well, the less said about that the better – but she liked not having to squeeze everything into evenings and weekends and in particular, not having to take time off work to sit in all day if there was a delivery or someone coming to look at the roof. She could relax at home knowing she wasn't wasting precious holiday AND in the knowledge that someone was doing her job, so there wouldn't find an enormous backlog when she went in again. And, truth be told, the work environment had been getting increasingly stressful. So many new things all the time and usually little or no warning before entirely new systems were put in place. She liked her work, though. It gave her a focus outside herself and an insight into other people's lives. Often, it provided her with the perspective she needed.

Maybe, with this current dilemma, she should check in with some of her colleagues over a coffee and see if she could get a different take on things.

***

'You know what, darling,' said Ross. 'I've given this a lot of thought and I really don't think there's any solution better than any other. So, you choose and I'll go along with whatever you decide.' Mia was momentarily taken aback. Once she'd marshalled her thoughts, she forgot all the recent deliberations and went with her original instinct. 'Perfect,' replied Ross. 'Let's get it going.'

She felt almost triumphant, so it was with a bump that she gazed at Ross from cloud nine and saw the beak and the grey feathers starting to sprout. 'Oh well,' she thought, 'they do say that if a thing appears to be too good to be true, it probably is.' And she got back to the task of sorting the washing.

Suffering gives
us a dark sense of
humour and some
dodgy coping
strategies

The inspiration for this came from a novel by Jenny Colgan.
Maggie and Stan were out for the evening and Maggie was dancing on the table, revelling in the fact that she could let her hair down after having to be a responsible adult all day in her teaching job. The moving picture of Alice threw into my head and this was the result.

TIME TO DANCE

'I'm twenty six, in the prime of my life. I can dance all night!'

The music was rushing through her veins, reaching the tips of her fingers and right down to her toenails. As her hips swirled and oscillated in response to the beat, her tongue tapped out the rhythm on the roof of her mouth. Her luxurious hair was describing patterns in the air. She had no inhibitions now. The music possessed her and moulded her in its own image. No longer the staid, sensible history teacher but a wild and unconstrained spirit, rejoicing in her own existence.

'Time for tea and biscuits, Alice,' said the nurse, a kind, comforting creature with a broad smile and gentle voice. 'Were you daydreaming?' she enquired.

'Dancing,' replied Alice. 'Middle Eastern. Wonderful stuff. It gets right into you and once you start moving, you can't stop.'

'It's a shame your dancing days are over,' said the nurse, handing over a cup of lukewarm tea and a soggy ginger nut.

'Yes it is,' agreed Alice, recalling the awkward, uncoordinated young woman feeling lonely and inadequate watching everyone else on the dance floor. 'Well,' she thought, 'Those days are over. Nothing can stop me now. Imagination can transport me anywhere I want to go.'

She ignored the tea and slipped back happily into her newfound abandon.

***

The nurse looked with affection at the silent, smiling face and stroked her hand. 'I'm so sorry I wasn't with you, Alice,' she said, a tear escaping down her cheek.

'It's fine,' she was sure she heard Alice whisper. 'The last thing I ever did was dance.'

She would never feel clumsy again.

*I start making my Christmas cards in July and
often wonder if it's really worth the effort.*

THE MOST WONDERFUL
TIME OF THE YEAR?

That time again.

Daisy looked at the display of cards spread around her. She wasn't one for waste and some of these cards were so beautiful, it would be a crime to chuck them out.

'I've only just done this,' she mused, remembering exactly the same scenario the year before. 'Where does the time go?' Knowing she'd never have the answer, she set to and got on with sorting out which ones she was going to use and who would be the correct recipient.

She cut the pictures from the ones she wanted to reuse and trimmed bits out of the others. She was never quite sure if she enjoyed this task every year. Making her Christmas cards was one of her personal traditions for the time of year but she couldn't help thinking it might have had its day. Whilst she loved the process, knowing she was creating something unique for every individual in her circle, she found it a bit tedious these days and – truth be told - a bit sad. Another year. Another cohort of friends and acquaintances who'd all vowed to meet up and 'not let it be so long next time'. It rarely happened though. How could it? Life moves on and keeping up with it proves difficult enough when addressing only the present issues, let alone resurrecting things that have passed. 'They've gone for a reason,' she told herself. 'Such things were just not meant to be.'

Inevitably, the nostalgia crept in as she sifted through all the messages and it occurred to her that within these cards was a very powerful symbolism. Reminders of all the wonderful people she'd known (and promises of those yet enter her life?), shared histories, support, love, laughter – 'I'm going through all this as if they're all consigned to the past. Why is Christmas always such a poignant time? Can't we just enjoy it?'

She picked up the first card to get started but instead of cutting out the picture, she opened it and read it again, the first time she'd done so in nearly a year. Or maybe it was the first time she'd ever read it, rather than opening it to see who it was from and then putting it in the display with all the others.

'Bob and the girls have gone to his mother's

this year. I'm spending it on my own. Can't be bothered with this charade anymore. Betty.'

She remembered intending to phone and find out what was going on to make her friend abandon her family but had never gotten around to it. 'Oh well,' she thought, 'I guess if anything important had happened, she'd have been in touch.' But there was a little niggle in the back of her mind that maybe she should have made more effort and that she'd definitely call Betty later today, knowing without consciously registering it that if she didn't do it this minute, it would get shelved again.

Every Christmas has its own story, she realised, beyond the universal practice of the giving and receiving of a gift or a card serving to remind us that we are remembered, that someone cares or at least, they did once, and enough to make it important to mark that memory. Affirmation that it was real not a fantasy borne of the passage of time. 'Or is it just habit?' she asked the universe. She recognised that rather than making the cards, she was ruminating so tried to get back to the task in hand but it just wouldn't happen. 'Better give in to the cogitations, then,' she thought, and made herself a coffee, which she took it into the conservatory to indulge the mood.

'Okay, let's list the positives. The one day of the year when it's quiet unless you choose to make it otherwise. After all, even the World Wars had a bit of respite on Christmas Day. Then of course, it's the day when we remember how to be rather than to do. Plus, remembering how we came to be who we are. The privilege of being alive, I guess.' This last one caused a welling up of tears, as so many of her circle weren't there anymore to share it all with. 'Mustn't dwell,' she decided. 'Okay. What are the downsides? Let's balance the two sides up and see which one wins. Nostalgia for things you had and can't have now.' She paused at this, again remembering those that could no longer have anything at all because they weren't around to have it. 'Oh dear. This is more painful than I thought it would be. Shall I just go and buy some cards from a charity shop?' But then the thought popped into her head that yes, there were lots of things she wanted that had gone forever but there were also loads of things she didn't want, had never wanted, that she'd never have again and was grateful for that. The notion cheered her considerably. 'That horrible job, for a start.' She thought back to all the hours lost to longing that the day would be over, so she could get on with the things she loved and be with people she cared about, not those she was thrown into contact with because of the need to pay the rent. 'Not so bad, after all,' she acknowledged, 'and the season itself is very beautiful, with some of the best music ever written dedicated to glories of the season. Can't be bad.'

She put on her coat and left the card making behind her, feeling she needed some fresh air and exercise to stop her increasingly melancholy train of thought; but even the gentle meander through the park, usually guaranteed to lift her spirits couldn't quell the stream of random thoughts – all the things that were here last year that weren't now, the people she'd neglected 'and who neglected me,' she thought, 'I'm not taking all the blame.' But then, was there any blame to be had? 'We just get on with life,' Betty told her once, 'Whatever it takes, Daise. Don't beat yourself up, Life's tough. Enjoy what you can and muddle your way through the rest,'

She changed her line of thinking to anticipation of the year to come but she'd lowered her mood so much that it just looked bleak. 'It'll only be more of the same,' she thought. 'Just when you think the water's under the bridge, it flows back again. Proof of the water cycle?' At this, she smiled to herself. 'At least I can still make a joke, however weak.'

Sitting on the bench overlooking the duck pond, her hand found its way into her pocket and when it emerged again, it was clutching her mobile phone. She dialled a number and waited for the reply.

'Betty?' she enquired, 'What gives?'

This Christmas was going to be better than she'd given it credit for.

If we see the world only through the clouded lens of our own perspective, we're done for.

G. K. Chesterton's
Father Brown

Like many people, I think of the birds in my garden as friends. Many of them come right up to the door and windows to be fed and one extremely cheeky robin pecks on the glass.

THE ROBIN

Lucy loved the robin, considering him to be her best friend. She knew he was him, because he sang all night, even during the winter. Sometimes she talked to him, telling him all about her daily life and asking him how, in the middle of February, he managed to survive without a 15 tog duvet and central heating; but he did and lucky for her that that was the case. He was such as tame visitor, she could hold out a handful of food and he'd hop onto it and feast until he'd cleared every crumb.

As she sat by the window, he hopped up

onto the windowsill, seemingly beckoning her to join him in the garden. What's he trying to tell me? she mused, as he scuttled backwards and forwards between her and the well-stocked bird table. He settled uneasily a few centimetres away from her face and looked at her intensely, cheeping at her with an urgency she didn't understand.

'What's the matter, little thing?' she asked him. From the corner of her eye, she could see another robin on the bare branch of the pear tree. 'Is he encroaching on your territory?' But no, he flew back to the branch and the two birds sat together in what appeared to be companionable silence. 'Ah,' she said, 'you've found a partner. Well done, little bird.'

His beckoning continued for several days, seeming to tell her 'if you stay indoors forever, you'll never find a mate'. He was right, of course, but it was so much safer and more comfortable in her cocooned little world. 'I'll enjoy your family instead,' she told him.

The robin had no time for her in the coming weeks, spending his time feeding his family, keeping her enthralled. In return, she protected him from cats and sparrowhawks and was amply rewarded with the addition of three fine robinets to her garden. Seeing his body raggedy from all his work, she was glad she'd helped him.

Late one afternoon, she settled down in her favourite armchair, happy in the knowledge that there was new life in her garden. She closed her eyes and drifted into a deep, contented sleep from which she never awoke.

In an earlier collection of stories*, Titania, Shakespeare's Queen of the Fairies in A Midsummer Night's Dream, made a swap with Lady Macbeth, so both could liven up their lives a bit. It worked for Lady M but sadly, not for poor Titania.

She's recently discovered that Gilbert and Sullivan's Iolanthe also has a Fairy Queen and approaches her to see if she, too, would like to try the swap.

This is the result.

*Wyddershyns, for any of you who would like to know.

ALL CHANGE

Titania:

Well, after that fiasco swapping with Lady M (I expect you remember - it turned out she wasn't a nice, respectable Scottish housewife at all, but a man-mad, sex-crazed harridan, possibly even a nutjob) who was after every man she could lay her hands on, including my lovely Oberon. So, I figured I'd stay in the background for a bit, be a good wife, do the cooking and cleaning and tend to all big O's needs. At least, I instructed all the relevant fairies to do so, and that's about the same thing, whatever he likes to claim. I even restricted my encounters with the gorgeous Cobweb, that's how serious I was about being faithful and loyal. Anyway, I have to admit to getting a bit bored after a bit. I mean, wouldn't you? Being upright and righteous is a fine calling. I'm not knocking it, not in the least, but it's much more appealing and worthy if it's someone else being the paragon and you can admire it at a distance, rather than being it yourself.

I found myself spending more and more time working out new perfume blends – it's ever so complicated, you know, and someone less cerebral than I would struggle – and, naturally, getting my nails manicured. I mean, I didn't want to let myself go, did I? That wouldn't do at all, even if Oby does think it's all an unnecessary indulgence for a fairy in my position, who should be 'setting an example'. What's wrong with the man? How much better an example could anyone set than keeping themselves nice? He'd soon point out my shortcomings if I let my hair go ratty or my figure get scraggy, even if he does prefer the company of gents, if you get my drift.

Anyway, one day, this Pumpkinblossom, who was curling my eyelashes for me, she said she'd been somewhere called the EEE NOE, where there was something called EYE- OWE- LANTHY and there was a fairy queen in it, just like me! Well, obviously not JUST like me, because I am THE Fairy Queen, the One That Matters, but all the same it got me to thinking: how about I flit up to Lunndunn and seek out this social climbing wannabe and see if she'd like to change places with me for a bit? I mean, this Eye-owe-lanthy's not really like the Bard at all, even if it is a theatre piece. It's music for a start, and everyone knows how accomplished I am at music and I don't get the chance to show that off in Willy's play. Some of the others do, but not me. Huh! And this Fairy Queen person sings most of the time and that's my special thing, so I thought this might be the perfect swap. You know what I mean, on the same level as me– well, not quite, I hear you all cry - but with all the same responsibilities weighing on her poor shoulders only she's not got Oberon pecking at her ears like his tongue's turned into a beak. Some people like him, you know. Lady M did. She was quite taken with him and it would seem him with her, but then he always did go for the big, butch types. I guess that's why he lost interest in me. As you know, I'm dainty and fairylike. No, not fairylike at all, because I AM a fairy, but feminine and caring with no thought for myself whatsoever No, this Fairy Queen is an unmarried lady and there are loads of human males around. I do so like a human male. So manly. And not demanding at all. Not for a highly charged fairy like I.

Of course, it took INCREDIBLE skill doing the swap. I was going into a different century where they have cars and everything and this EEE NOE wasn't like the usual places we MSD fairies work in, what with lots of people playing instruments we don't have in Fairyland. But, as you are all aware, I'm persistent and focussed and I thought very long and hard, even for a fairy (long enough to have got my toe nails polished, had I wanted to, THAT's how long) and figured it couldn't be any more difficult than transforming myself into a diligent housewife for the Macbeth fellow or even for Oberon come to that, because I'm not really the wifey type. So, I took to the wing and ended up in St Martin's Lane. The adventure was underway!

Fairy Queen:

It's rather nice here in Fairyland, although I was very apprehensive before I came. It's not at all what I'm used to and had no idea what to expect, so every instant brings something new and exciting with novel experiences at every turn.

Where I come from, we're singers, not fairies at all, and that's what opera's all about – singing good music and dressing up so we can convince the audience we're not ourselves. If you can keep a secret – I didn't even realise that there was such a thing as a real fairy, so I was very dubious when

I got the communication from someone claiming to be Titania. I'd heard of her, of course. Everyone has. She's one of the few major female roles in Shakespeare's canon and there's a great part for her in Britten's opera, but I never realised she was real. I thought Shakespeare had made her up. Well, there we are. Never too late to learn.

All the same, after a great deal of thought it seemed it might be good to have a go at the swap she suggested. It might even spice up my life a bit. I love my job, honestly I do, but seven times a week can be a bit hard going. Added to which, there's a guy in the band I've had my eye on for yonks but he's not interested in me, so I thought getting away to try something different might help me get over him.

Iolanthe – for you who don't know it – it's a pleasant enough operetta as they go, and stands the test of time better than most but I've sung this role since I was a student and I've got a bit jaded. I yearn to sing something avante garde, test new boundaries, maybe have a go at the odd soprano role, Britten's Titania even; but I doubt that'll ever happen. Still, this swap might give me a way in.

So, she organised it all and I found myself standing in for her. Officially, I'm Oberon's wife. As nice as he is, I see why she wasn't that interested. He's more interested in the boys – nothing unusual in that but if it's a man you want with all that a man can provide, it's not much help if he prefers his own kind. He goes off a lot to prove himself macho, so she's banging around on her own in that enormous fairy castle more than could be considered healthy. So, you can feel a bit more sympathy for poor Titania

– or Titty, as he calls her – what with her being left to her own devices far too much of the time. And truly, it doesn't take much to understand what she finds appealing about these fairy men. It's doing me the world of good having them around and I haven't thought longingly once about the fiddle player at the ENO. No time.....

Titania:

Well, I always come off worst. Moan, moan, moan, that's all they do. 'I miss Iolanthe', 'Where's Iolanthe', 'Why can't we get Iolanthe back?' Good grief. She's only a fairy, when all's said and done. And the men! They're all human men and I'm rather partial, as, it would seem, was this Iolanthe. It got her banished to the bottom of a river. What's wrong with that, you ask, but apparently in this world living on a river bed is Bad News. I'm getting off the point. So: do you know what? All the chaps are great hulking beasts wandering about in scratchy robes

and coronets like the world belongs to them and everyone else owes them a living! And the singing. Not that great after all, not if you're a real fairy, rather than a made up one. They're not lovely tinkly songs about the thyme and eglantine. Oh dear me no. They're all this nonsense about tripping hither and thither and some rather portly chap being a member of Parlyment, whatever that might be, and the dullest stuff about having headaches because you can't sleep and passing bills and frankly, you can't begin to imagine how gross it all is. And then there's Private Willis. Now, he's not so bad, not really. He has quite a good figure with muscles and a lean frame; and he's got patience and endurance and that's something a woman admires, but really, what's the point of someone who does nothing but stand in a sentry box all the time? I mean, he seemed TOTALLY immune to my not inconsiderable charm and wouldn't budge, not until the end and then it was only because there was no-one else available. And then there's the song they gave me! All about a fireman and how the right thing would be for someone to come along and dampen the Queen's ardour because after all, she has to control herself, what with being a queen and honestly, what a load of utter tosh! If you want the company of a gentleman, you just get on and get it together. I guess Oberon would like it though. He doesn't really approve of what he calls polly-ammery, not in me anyway, even though he sees no reason why he shouldn't practice it himself.

To make matters worse, there's this chap in what they call the Pit who keeps on leering at me and he cornered me one night and asked me why I wasn't singing as well as usual, did I have a cold or sore feet and how about we get together for a drink after the show! So I told him straight, my singing is just fine, thank you very much, and I have no interest in getting together with you after the show for a drink or anything else and he said 'Pity, I thought you had the hots for me' and I thought 'how coarse!' and flew off but then I was a bit sad, because he was rather attractive and no-one else was taking much notice.

I expect you'll think I'd been through enough, but on top of all that, it seems that some bloke called Ben made up music to go with Bill's play and there's a big bit in it for me, singing and everything, and no-one's ever told me, so that was ANOTHER blow. I mean, I AM TITANIA and I should have been told. No, I SHOULD have been ASKED but it seems I'm not even on the radar.   How did I ever find myself in this position?

Fairy Queen:
The landscapes, sunrises, the sound of the colours – truly, they have a voice here – and the stunning patterns made in the air! Speaking of the music – it's absolutely divine and like nothing I've ever heard! I woke up this morning to the accompaniment of an oh-so-delicate percussion orchestra playing something like the song of a blackbird transmuted into a four part choral anthem. It wrapped me up like a sonic duvet and it was all coming from nowhere! I can sing everything I've ever dreamed of and things I'd never even begun to imagine! No need to worry about range or timbre, it's all just there to be called on anytime you want

it. No need even to practice! If I didn't know it was Fairyland, I'd think it was heaven. Oh this glorious life! It's just wonderful!

The fairygirls are lovely, with their happy laughter and chattering and never a cross word. They took me flying through the sweet pea tunnel earlier and the scent would have been overwhelming, except that nothing seems to be too much for the senses to luxuriate in here. And the fairymen – well, it gets more obvious by the second why Titania isn't content to stick just with Oberon. He really is a bit of a bore and the rest of them are such a delight. Mind you, they all call me Your Gracious Majesty and try to be deferent to me and I don't like that at all, but I've told them, no ceremony, no special treatment. Treat me exactly like you do each other. They seem to find it a little odd, not treating me like a queen but how could I want them to? Being here, when every moment is enchantment, is enough.

The only tiny drawback is that you only have to think of something and it happens, which means you really do need to be careful what you wish for and it takes a little time to adjust but honestly, if you ever get the chance to try it out, do!

Titania:

Oh lord, there goes the wretched bell. Back to the dressing room to get ready for another night of it. Duty calls…

ACKNOWLEDGEMENTS

Special thanks to Barry Ecuyer,
Peter Fry and Dave Whistance

Also to:

Linda Colin

James Lycett

Cheryl May

Steve at Paxman Horns

Ros Whistance

and to

Linda, Cheryl, Norton, Tim, Maureen,
David, Martin, Tony C, Mali, Peter L, Peter,
Stephen, Helen, John, Tony R, Sera, Martin S,
Wendy, James, Jane
– for helping to shape the person I am.

WYDDERSHYNS
Unexpected life stories

In this collection of reminiscences and short stories, Polly J. Fry creates whole worlds in bite sized chunks. Each selection of tales is punctuated by a memoir from Fry's life, paying tribute to the people who shared the good times and guided her – unknowingly – through difficult times. The stories range from the everyday adventures of the wonderfully engaging Mrs Khan through to science fiction, mystery and romance. Fry even reimagines some of Shakespeare's characters, who decide to swop plays, the consequences leading to a myriad twists and turns.

There's something here for everyone.

MRS KHAN AND THE W.I. BUCKET LIST

The indomitable Mrs Khan has really started something. The members of the Stackton-on-Sea Women's Institute are determined to help each other achieve their dreams. With this in mind they're created a Bucket List.

There's **Val**, adapting to being a first-time newly-wed in her retirement years,

Dorothy, set on a visit to a cocoa bean plantation,

Lally, sorting out a future for her and her little daughter Chelsea

And

Helena, going for a career on the stage.

And who is The Wizard?

Come along and see how they get on.

VOICES

Polly J. Fry was a singer. Acting on an extremely foolish whim, she damaged her voice and for sixteen years was unable to sing.

Voices is a three-part narrative exploring the process of accepting that her singing voice was gone, the even greater trauma of rebuilding it once it had resurfaced; and the years in between.

Interspersed through the autobiographical story are bite-sized fictional tales set in vividly-painted microworlds – Fry's signature format. The exploits of the delightful, if somewhat extraordinary, Grannie Louie contrast with stories of drama, romance and comedy; the everyday stories of ordinary people.

Fry's own story is very different from the one she'd expected to write. Nonetheless, her honesty and candour in describing her experiences reveal a tale well worth telling, full of hope and optimism.

A worthy successor to Wyddershyns.

AM I MY VOICE?

This is the narrative relating the adjustments necessary when Fry found herself unable to sing and subsequently started to find her voice again. Originally appearing in a truncated version in Voices, it gives an update on progress and makes an appeal for greater understanding of voice loss, whether the individual concerned is a professional voice user or not.

Printed in Great Britain
by Amazon

36464871R00089